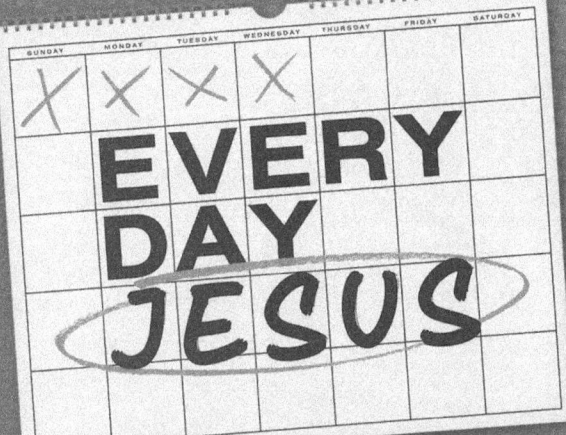

NATHAN KING

CONTENTS

Introduction ix

1. With Us 1
2. We All Follow 7
3. Here and Now 17
4. Wrong Turns 23
5. Satisfied 31
6. The Cost 43
7. The Better Savior 53
8. Up A Hill 61
9. On A Hill 71
10. Under Your Mask 81
11. Run Together 91
12. Heroes and Villains 101
13. A Bad Friend 111
14. The Fog 121
15. Forty Eight Hours 129
16. Home 137
17. Delight 147
18. Beating Temptation 159
19. Make It Simple 165
20. Everything 175
21. Live the Story 183
22. Pray Like Jesus 195
23. Love and Noise 205
24. Good Fruit 219
25. Proof 231
    Conclusion 241
    Also by Nathan King 245
    About The Author 247

Everyday Jesus

Copyright © 2023, Nathan King

Published by NK Solutions, LLC.

All rights reserved. Printed in the United States of America. No part of this book may be used, reproduced in any manner, stored in a retrieval system, or transmitted in any form by any means—electronic, mechanical, photocopy, recording, or otherwise—without prior written permission of the author, except in the case of brief quotations embodied in critical articles and reviews, or as provided by United States of America copyright law.

Edited by Rachael Bernardi

Cover design by Drew Roberts, Roberts Creative Inc.

ISBN: 978-1-7374691-8-6

eBook: 978-1-7374691-9-3

For Uncle David & Aunt JoAnn.
They lived it everyday.

INTRODUCTION

"I need help," the young soldier told me with tears in his eyes. "Can you help me?" The tears continued to roll down his face as we stood in the church lobby, with hundreds of people streaming past us on their way to lunch.

The brilliant, capable young man stood before me in anguish. Who could say no to someone in such turmoil?

"I can help you," I told him.

I prayed for him right where we stood. We exchanged phone numbers, and I promised to meet up with him later that week. When Friday morning rolled around, we were sitting across from each other downtown in an old train car transformed into a cafe.

Roger began to open up to me about his recent struggles. He had left a trail of broken relationships and bad habits behind him. He had a tide of uncertain outcomes rolling toward him. He found himself at a crossroads and was looking for someone who could help him take his next step.

We talked about his childhood. He had two loving parents who were still together after many years. We talked about his plans for the future. He was excelling in his role in the military and hoped to make a career out of it. As we talked about his faith, the crux of Roger's struggles came to light.

Roger had grown up going to church with his parents. That is, until some over-eager religious folks did some idiotic stuff, leaving his dad fed up with church. Roger's dad never looked back. He left the church behind. He left Jesus behind. And he left his young son behind just as the boy was trying to find out what role Jesus would have in his life.

The spiritual abandonment left Roger wandering during his formative years. When he was trying to look to his father for help—his dad had hung a "closed" sign on the door to his heart. That would be hard for anyone, but it's especially hard for a young man with a strong sense of justice, hoping for a hand from the most important man in his life.

Once his dad checked out, Roger's life flew into a tailspin of bad habits. His life reflected his father's struggle. Roger believed deeply in Jesus. He believed Jesus was the Son of God. But he didn't know what that was supposed to mean everyday.

Roger didn't know how or even if Jesus fit into his relationships. He didn't know how much Jesus wanted to be part of his future plans. He didn't understand how much Jesus valued and treasured the man he was becoming. He didn't know where to turn to find the answers his young heart was yearning for.

In his heart, he wanted to believe. He desperately wanted it. He had been holding on to hope.

His story laid out before me, Roger sighed. "See how messed up I am?"

I gave him my best smile. I was full of so much hope for him. But I knew what I wanted for Roger was only a drop in the bucket compared to what Jesus had for him.

So I made Roger a promise. It's the same promise I've lived by for years now. It's the promise that changed my life more than thirty years ago. It's the promise I've tried to help people understand for over twenty-five years. It's the best promise anyone can know who is struggling to find their footing regarding faith, habits, choices, relationships, and so many of life's opportunities.

"Every day with Jesus is better than any day without him."

WHAT JESUS WANTS

Way too many people are living a life like the one Roger struggled with. Until he realized that Jesus is an Everyday Jesus. Until Roger realized Jesus wasn't a Sunday thing. He came to understand Jesus wanted to be part of his everyday life. Jesus wants the same thing for you.

So many people are living life without Jesus. Maybe

they go to church on Sunday to check some kind of religious, cultural, or familial obligation off their list. It's like going to the gym once a year and hoping for a six-pack. Most don't even do that. Most people just ignore Jesus altogether.

How does Jesus influence your daily life? If you are living without him, you are missing what he wants for you. In fact, he died so your life could be different.

Perhaps the reality of your present situation is that your life is not influenced by Jesus. You go to work without him. You navigate your home life and essential relationships without him. Even your habits and hobbies are missing what he wants for you. If that describes you, you're missing the piece that holds it all together.

The simple truth is this: *Jesus loves you.* A life lived without him is much less than what it could be. If that's you—you're right where Roger was. Embrace the promise Roger came to realize. Jesus is an Everyday Jesus. And, everyday with Jesus is better than any day without him.

When you do, you will treat the people around you differently. Your relationships will become better than you ever dreamed they could be. When Jesus becomes part of your everyday reality, you will treat yourself differently, too. Your personal habits will shift. Your emotional well-being will improve. You will find peace and joy inside. Your strength to face your struggles will come from someone who wants nothing but the best for you.

Living everyday with Jesus shouldn't be complicated. It should be simple and straightforward. Life with Jesus should be personal. Life with Jesus should be full of grace. Life with Jesus should be full of purpose.

If you have struggled with any of those things, it's time to disrupt the status quo. It's time to walk away from where you've been. It's time to move into the kind of life Jesus has always wanted for you. The life where he is. It's time to embrace Jesus everyday.

When I set out to write this book, it was for a very specific person and purpose. My big audacious dream for this book is that it will land in the hands of someone like Roger. Someone who wants to live everyday in the company of Jesus. Someone willing to reach out and ask for help.

My prayer for every page has been that it will all point to a single guiding principle. Jesus. Always. You can skip around if something in the table of contents grabs your attention. But the order is intentional and, I hope, helpful.

There are chapters about the character and nature of Jesus as he has revealed himself to me over the years. Because why would anyone want to spend everyday with someone if they don't know them? Who Jesus is informs a lot about where we go and how we get there with him.

Some of the chapters are about some of the bumps in the road we'll all face. You can't go anywhere without facing some challenges. Every journey involves an intersection or two. These chapters address some of the most common issues I've encountered in my own life and in twenty-five years of trying to help others sort it out for themselves.

Ultimately, I aim to provide a set of tools that will equip you to truly live out your faith authentically everyday. I want to help you realize how simple life with Jesus is. I want you to know how much freedom there is. I hope you will come away full of hope. I want your heart to fill up with the kind of hope Jesus has for you. I want you to realize what it looks like when grace is part of your everyday rhythm. I want you to find purpose. One that surges inside you daily as you walk hand in hand with Jesus—everyday.

You'll learn what Roger, myself, and countless others have discovered across the ages: Everyday with Jesus is better than any day without him.

CHAPTER 1
WITH US

EVERYDAY

Roger looked across the table at me with a contemplative look, almost as if he was trying to remember if he'd left his oven on at home. I could tell my promise was still bouncing around in his mind, but I was hoping it would take root in his heart.

"Roger, I've met so many young men and women like you over the years." I began. "People God loves who don't know what to do about it. They think all this 'Jesus stuff' is really good on Sunday; but don't let it affect the rest of their week." We all need to learn and remember what Roger needed to grasp.

Jesus is an Everyday Jesus. He loves you. He has a plan for your life. And it is not limited to one day of the week when you wear nice clothes, go sing some Christian version of karaoke, and listen to a big personality give a faith-based Ted Talk.

God's plan for your life is so much bigger than planned worship services in air-conditioned buildings. It's more important than our organizations, agendas, and issues. Jesus is about the business of extending invitations. He offers an invitation to a life that is rich in love, purpose, forgiveness, and so much more.

The invitation Jesus extended to us was not a one-time thing. It's an everyday opportunity. And we need it.

Jesus isn't some cosmic party pooper. He's not the guy who'll take away your ice cream because there's too much sugar. Jesus isn't trying to squeeze all the fun out of our lives. He isn't trying to turn us into prudish zombies. He offers a way to live that is fulfilling in purpose, unique in application, and full of freedom across the board.

Jesus wants you in his kingdom. To do that, he wants into your life. He wants to be with you, not just on the highlight reel days but also on those "I spilled coffee on my shirt" days. Because, let's face it, those happen a lot more than we'd like to admit.

WITH US

In the Bible story, an angel appeared to Mary—probably giving her the biggest shock of her life—to let her know she'd won the cosmic genetic lottery. She was going to be a mom. The mother of the Son of God.

The angel gave a directive. He said that the baby would be called "Emmanuel," but this isn't a book about Everyday Emmanuel. Or is it? The directive the angel was offering wasn't about names. It was about more than that. Emmanuel means "God with us".

God had taken the form of a baby to come to those he loved so much. Jesus is Emmanuel. Jesus is God with us.

He wants to be with us. Everyday. He wants to be with you. Everyday. Jesus wants to be with you in the grocery store, but probably not because he wants to point out that those cookies you're eyeballing aren't on your diet. He wants to be there helping you in the boardroom. He's probably chuckling when you think your muted Zoom call hides your pajama bottoms. He hopes you'll take him with you on the subway or the next time you catch an Uber. Jesus wants to be with you at home, work, and play. He wants to be with you. Why? Because Jesus is an Everyday Jesus.

How? Well, that's what this book is really about. But why would Jesus want such a prominent role in our lives? Why would Jesus want to hang out with us so much? Is it because he likes our style? I don't think so. Perhaps he's a big fan of human hobbies? No. That's not it. It's because of how much we mean to Him. Why should Jesus be so important to us? Because of how important we are to Him. He loves you so much. He values you. He treasures you.

ONE

Every person who has experienced the incredible grace of God flood their life knows what it's like to be valued. A first-century historian named Luke wrote down many of the stories Jesus told. Several of them highlight the importance placed on you when you were far from God. They serve as an incredible reminder of why he went through all that he did. Because you were valued. You are valued.

Luke also captured the idea that angels celebrate the moment someone decides to live everyday with Jesus. It is a celebration like none other. And if you have become a follower of Christ, there are still echoes of rejoicing reverberating through the halls of eternity.

One of my favorite things to learn about someone who shares my faith is how they came to it. The stories are as different and varied as the people I meet and ask. I've met people who were compelled to find God after they reached their life's biggest dream, and it came up empty. I've known others who watched all they had ever loved go down the drain because of their reckless choices—and at rock bottom, they looked up to see Jesus had been searching for just such an opportunity to show them his love.

Jesus is always looking for the next one who will accept His love. Jesus is always waiting and ready for someone willing to turn their life around. Only when we step into the loving relationship God wants for us do we begin to live out the potential always there waiting.

It's not instant. It's a start. The party the angels throw is about all of the good things that will come from what is taking place when a lost son or daughter comes home to our Good Father.

TOUCHDOWN

I grew up in church and was no stranger to Jesus as a kid. But one week before my twelfth birthday, I accepted Jesus's invitation to be part of my life everyday. It happened at the end of a gathering my community had thrown on our local high school football field.

Now, I've never played a single down of football in my life. I was younger and smaller than everyone growing up. But Jesus said Heaven has a party when someone decides to spend everyday with Jesus. On a Tuesday night in a small town endzone, I knelt and prayed. Heaven rejoiced! It's the closest thing I've ever come to a touchdown.

Everyone who has experienced the love of Christ in their life has a moment in their story just like mine. A moment when Heaven gasped in excitement and celebrated in full. But not everyday feels like a party, even with Jesus.

In the more than thirty years since that day, I've lived through all of the worst days of my life. Heartache, pain, loss, sin, destructive habits, reckless choices, and a litany of bad things that chose me. None of them felt like a party.

If you've lived through hard things, you probably know the feeling. It's the tension between swinging for the home run and striking out, like running out of gas when you're on your way to the most important appointment of the day.

On days like those, it's easy for me to be my biggest critic. But I need to remember my value. It's vital to remember who values me.

You are loved. You are wanted. You are cherished. You were grafted into Heaven's family by Jesus himself. Who you are is summed up by whose you are—and you're more than enough.

On those days when it doesn't seem so, or when something says otherwise, the voice that's telling you you're loved, you're forgiven, you're a Child of God can be hard to hear. Still your heart and your soul. Turn off the cell phone. Go for a short drive. Maybe just take a walk.

When everything gets quiet, remember this phrase: "I am celebrated. I am loved. I am His." Why? Because your life, your soul, and your purpose carry value before God. Jesus wants you to spend everyday with him.

CHAPTER 2
WE ALL FOLLOW

ALL FOLLOW

If you're a parent, you have probably had a child try to follow you out of the house. One day, my son screamed, "But I want to go with you!" from the top of the stairs as I was headed out the front door. I could hear him crying as I got into my car. The discomfort of that moment tugs on a dad's heart. If you are a parent, you already know what I'm talking about. You have lived it.

If you love someone, you want them to go with you. It's that simple. We want to be with people we love. We almost always recognize this even if it seems impossible in some circumstances. So why is it so hard to nail this when following Jesus?

We all follow someone. I want to follow Jesus. I want to follow him in every aspect of my life. I've been trying to do that for a long time now. You're reading this, so chances are pretty good you do, too. We want to follow Jesus. But we must acknowledge that the distance between our desire and behavior is often greater than we'd like. Why? Because stuff seems to get in the way.

Think about that for a moment. You have this desire to follow Jesus with your life, but it conflicts with your everyday circumstances. In other words, some obstacles get in the way. Impediments that keep us from following Jesus well.

Following Jesus is the best way to live. Only following Jesus leads us somewhere good. Only following Jesus leads us to someone good. But everyone is following something or someone.

Many things that people follow are not good. Many people follow their stuff. They go in search of external satisfaction. This happens when we think something we can attain will satisfy us. They chase possessions, a bigger and better home, a faster car, and more toys. This leads to debt, the rat race, comparison, envy, and more. They chase pleasure, even though following pleasure can never satisfy them in the long run. Following stuff is about worshiping *satisfaction*.

Many other people are following feelings in search of internal justification. This happens when we think something we can do will make us better. So they chase status, notoriety, worth, and self-esteem. This often leads to becoming a workaholic, falling into depression, fixating on selfishness, or something equally destructive.

It's a dogged pursuit of wanting to be "okay with

ourselves," "feel good about ourselves," or whatever. Following feelings is about worshiping ourselves. These are dangerous ways to live!

It's critical to consider. What are you following? Because we are all following something.

The stakes here are huge because what you follow is what you worship. I don't want to worship stuff. I don't want to chase the bigger house or the nicer car. Not because those things are bad. There is nothing wrong with having nice stuff. I like my stuff. I'll probably buy more stuff this week. But the stuff in our lives will control our lives if we allow it.

I don't want to worship feelings and accolades. I am going to keep working hard. I have three jobs right now. And I don't care one bit about titles. I'd be okay if no one ever called me "Pastor Nate" again. No one has to call me "Professor King" at school. In fact, I ask them not to. Why? Because I'm not chasing accolades and feelings.

The danger of following our stuff and our feelings is that they make pretty terrible gods. Because ultimately, it means we are worshiping ourselves. What you follow is what you worship.

BLIND RELIGION

Jesus developed a bad reputation among the religious people of his day. But the everyday dudes like you and me liked him. Crowds gathered around Jesus. Tradesmen laid down their tools and followed him.

Why? They learned firsthand what Jesus wants you and I to take to heart. Everyday with Jesus is better than any day without him.

The religious folks didn't like Jesus. In fact, they murdered him. He got a bad reputation because he "hung out with tax collectors and sinners". He ignored the man-made religious rules and only honored God's law. This especially ticked them off. Jesus made life with God simple. He penetrated the religious bureaucracy, calling its cosmic bluff with every offense.

The religious guys followed their rules—not God. Well, guess who made the rules? They did. They worshiped themselves and played like they were worshiping God. When Jesus showed up, many of them started "following" him. They would cause trouble, ask questions, and ridicule his teaching in front of crowds.

So, one day, Jesus called them out in front of the crowd. Jesus spoke blatantly out of his authority as the Son of God, saying "These people give me lip service, but not their hearts. They are full of vanity, following human rules."

What was Jesus saying? You can't follow him with only words. Following Jesus has to be more than lip service.

Being a follower of Jesus is about more than a prayer. People pray a token prayer and then act like there's nothing else to it. That's a really disastrous way to live. Jesus doesn't want us to follow him by going through the motions. Jesus wants us to follow him with our life. I'm not talking about moralism. I'm not talking about pursuing a bunch of man-made ideas. I'm not talking about religious duty or rules. That's the junk the people who hated Jesus focused on. You know, the ones who murdered him.

Jesus called those guys "blind guides." He encouraged the crowds to leave behind their blind guides as they followed him. He told them, "If the blind lead the blind, both will fall into a pit." What makes it extra spicy is that Jesus so often went out of his way to heal blind people. I'm probably wrong, but I'd like to think he turned and gave the religious guys a stare-down every time he healed another blind guy.

If you're following man-made stuff, you're blind. You're following the blind. You're still living in the dark. You can't follow Jesus and live in the dark. He's the light of the world.

One night as a kid, I was running through a friend's yard. We were playing tag in the dead of night. There was no moonlight that night. It was pitch black, and we didn't have any lights. It was dangerous. In other words, it was the perfect little hillbilly game. I was sprinting and stepped off a sidewalk into blackness, right into a ditch four feet deep. I literally never saw it coming. I was so lucky I didn't get hurt.

Plenty of people are blindly following the blind. They follow the outrage culture because it makes them feel good. They follow some politician because he says just the right things. They follow a singer or actor because they like their style. They follow some writer because he is so witty or intelligent. They may follow a buddy who has a few answers or some mom who makes cool videos on social media; but none of those are Jesus. It's the blind leading the blind.

I was a college pastor for over fifteen years. Each year, we had an event called Battle of the Sexes. We would divide into teams of guys versus girls and play a bunch of games.

Looking back, I realized one of the games was so dangerous. We would blindfold the whole team, and one person would lay on a stretcher. Then, the blindfolded folks would carry the person on the stretcher. The one on the stretcher had to talk their team through an obstacle course as they raced the other team to the finish line. It was a blast, but it only worked because someone could see.

If we aren't following Jesus, who are we following? We are following the blind. We are chasing the dark.

COME WITH ME

We need Jesus today. We need him everyday. We need him to rescue us from our own destructive behavior. We need him to help us reject our shame, shortcomings, and condemnation. We need him to help us focus our lives on something good and noble. We need him to help us love those around us. We need him to carry us forward in purpose.

One of the best examples is Jesus' interaction with a guy named Levi. Jesus saw Levi working one day and said, "Come along with me." Levi had let work get in the way. He was collecting taxes.

Sometimes, we are influenced from the outside in ways we don't even realize. One day, we may look up and realize we've taken too many steps down a different path. How does this happen? It happens because of our everyday choices and decisions.

Even good things can lead to a life that goes off the tracks. Obligations can become obstacles when we aren't diligent. Diligent about what? About what God wants for you.

It's not like it's a big secret. Jesus wants you to follow him. He invites you to follow him. He compels each of us to follow him.

Jesus takes our shame, so we will follow him shamelessly! His selfless sacrifice is the invitation into the remarkable—a life spent following the Son of God. Jesus lived and died to make a clear path for us to follow. He calls everyone to follow him. And we have to choose how to answer that call.

We see this in the story of Jesus calling Levi. Tax collectors were hated by their fellow Jews. They were seen as traitors. They were corrupt. They extorted their countrymen. Yet Jesus looked at Levi and said, "Come with me."

If you feel like you've gone too far or messed up too much, it's never too late to follow Jesus. Why? Because He wants you to go with him. If you've committed your life to Christ, you want to go with him.

Which is why it's crazy and confusing when we realize we aren't doing it very well. Mistakes are inevitable. Distractions are abundant. Perfection lies far outside our reach. But that's okay. Not because we're actively looking to self-destruct. It's okay, because he never expected us to ace it all of the time. He loves it when I ask for his help.

Jesus wants us to follow him. Jesus wants us to hear his heartfelt words declaring, "Come with me". Upon hearing these words, he hopes we will begin to take our first baby steps in an eternity of following Him.

When I'm playing in the yard with my kids, there's a significant difference between how my eight-year-old son can follow me and my eighteen-month-old daughter. Ethan can run, play, ride bikes, and be adventurous. Anna tries to run, too. And she falls a lot. There are big differences in the way my kids follow me. One of the main differences is the size of the things that impede them. Ethan might shrug at the waist-high grass if we're at the family farm. While to Anna, it would seem like an insurmountable green wall.

As we grow in Christ, the impediments change. The hurdles change. A person following Jesus closely for thirty years may not have the same struggles as someone who was just introduced to him. Following Jesus everyday leads to change, but not perfection. There will always be something trying to trip you up. There will always seem to be something else in the way. There's always the next choice, the next fork in the road, the next potential disaster, or the next hurdle.

Parents try hard to keep their kids from experiencing this, but God doesn't seem to do it that way. Why? It's because He knows what we get to learn. Hurdles aren't disasters. They are part of the race. We're supposed to embrace what we learn from the impediments. Take them in stride.

Jesus didn't consider the cross and the discomforts of the road as disqualifying experiences. They were hard, sure. But they made it worth it. What He offers each of us is the opportunity to walk in His love and grace. Not free of fault, but in spite of it.

What happens as we follow Jesus? He takes us on the adventure of a lifetime. One that changes everything when we're willing to go where he went and do what he did.

WHAT NOW?

Followers of Jesus walked where he walked. When we follow Jesus closely, we walk where He walked. Our life takes us into contact with people needing God's love. We have a better sense for where our next step should land.

We used to ask, "What would Jesus do?" Everybody wore bracelets declaring "WWJD" when I was in high school. It is *the question* when it comes to following Jesus.

Decide to follow Jesus closely. There's a good chance you'll get tripped up along the way. When you do, you'll bump into Him all over again. Walk where He walked.

Followers of Jesus love whom Jesus loved. When we walk where Jesus walked, we find the opportunity to love those Jesus loved. Those who are rejected, broken, and in need. Not know-it-alls, but the down-and-outs. We all love a comeback story because we are a comeback story. Following him is our opportunity to add to the story.

Follow Jesus closely. Walk where He walked. Love who He loved. Give what He gave.

Followers of Jesus give what Jesus gave. Faced with the ones Jesus loves, I am presented with an opportunity to give what He gave—myself. All of us have to choose this. It might mean we give our time, our resources, our attention, or any number of things. Mostly, it means we give what we can.

This is the kind of life Jesus has invited us into: one that follows closely. Loving who He loved. Giving what He gave. When I'm getting it right, I have a better sense of where my next step should land. If I have let distance creep in, it might be harder to understand how He wants me to take the next corner.

When you walk where He walked, you'll always find yourself moving in the right direction. Your life goes in new directions. When you love who He loved, you'll always find yourself surrounded by people who need Jesus. Your life has a new mission. When you give what He gave, you'll never stop living from the abundance of God's big plan for life. What could be better than that?

CHAPTER 3
HERE AND NOW

GOOD NEWS

One day, my son blurted out, "Daddy, I have some bad news." I thought he would tell me something no parent wants to hear. Like, "I don't love you anymore." Or "I want to play golf."

I was like, "What is it, buddy?" He had this super serious look. "I left my library book at school." Whew! I was so relieved! In his world, that was bad news. Thank God for the innocence of kids!

Last year, I had a friend look at my house because we were just about to put it up for sale. He asked, "Do you want the bad news or the really bad news?" No, I'm kidding. He didn't say that! That would have been terrible. He said what we are all used to hearing in a conversation like that: "Do you want the good news or the bad news?"

Which do you like to hear first: the good news or the

bad news? That's a no-brainer, right? Who wants to listen to the good news first and leave on a sour note? If you're someone who likes bad news first, well, I have bad news for you–you're weird.

The truth is we live in a world full of bad news. Sometimes, our life is even split into two parts by bad news. Here are some examples from my own journey. There was life before my nephew died and life after. There was life before my brother's cancer and life after.

What bad news changed things for you? Maybe it was a lost loved one. Perhaps it was a terrible diagnosis. For some of you, it was finding out a loved one betrayed you. Bad news can shake us to our core. It is personal. It is tragic. And it is real. Terrible things happen all over the world every day. But it is not the end of the story. If you focus on it too much, it will consume you.

Bad news always boils down to one of three things. Something was stolen–like property or an opportunity. Something was killed–like a person, group, or dream. Something was destroyed–like a natural disaster. Or Johnny Depp's acting career. When something is stolen, killed, or destroyed. It can be devastating. It can be a tragedy. But it's not the end of the story.

Here's some good news. It is *the Good News*. Everyday with Jesus is better than any day without him because Jesus changes everything.

In the bible, the stories about Jesus are kicked off by a guy named Matthew. He was a dude whose story begins as a scam artist and overall crook, but he became someone else. Matthew became a guy willing to die for Jesus. He went from being willing to rob his neighbors blind to being willing to lay down his very life. What changed? Matthew encountered the Good News: everyday with Jesus is better than any day without him.

Matthew had experienced a lot of bad, and then he met Jesus. Matthew discovered Jesus changes everything. He even staked his very life on this idea. He was killed because of it. But Matthew's journey with Jesus started with something we're all challenged with.

One day, Jesus was hanging out with his friends when he encountered Matthew in his everyday routine. There Matthew was, sitting at his workstation, his authorized tax spot where he robbed his neighbors. Jesus saw Matthew. Matthew saw Jesus. He had to know who Jesus was. By then, Jesus had a pretty big reputation. Jesus looked at Matthew and gave the best sermon in human history, "Follow me." And Matthew did. He got up and followed.

In one move, Matthew swapped being with the ancient Roman IRS to being with Jesus. He traded being in the mob for being a disciple. He'd gone from hurting the people to helping the people. With two words, Jesus changed everything, "Follow me."

Jesus changes everything—being with Jesus changes everything. When you follow Jesus, he restores who you were meant to be.

FOR YOU

After Matthew decided to follow Jesus, the whole gang wound up at his house for dinner. Something tells me that's not what Matthew had in mind, but it's a great picture. Many people I've known who say they plan to follow Jesus seem a little surprised when they find out he wants to hang out at their house. Sometimes I think it's because we're a little bummed by what we think he'll discover if we let him get close. Other times I think we realize letting Jesus on the inside of our lives means putting out some things that have commanded our affections. This isn't because Jesus demands perfection but because his love is too big to share space with anything trying to keep us from following him.

When Jesus showed up for supper at Matthew's house, many other tax collectors and people like us showed up to eat, too. They're called sinners. Some cranky religious guys saw what was happening and started interrogating the other disciples. Their line of questioning was pretty simple, but it's also essential for you and me to understand. They wanted to know one thing. Why does Jesus hang out with broken people?

Have you ever wondered why God did something? It's an innocent enough question when we're being curious. I'm not convinced the cranky religious guys in the story were curious. I think their question was accusing. It seems they were questioning Jesus' motives, but Jesus' reason was simple. He saw people who had spent a lot of days without him. Everyone needs to experience their first day with Jesus before they can live everyday with Jesus.

Jesus was pretty pointed with the religious guys. In his own way he said, "I didn't come for the people like you who think they have it all figured out. I came for the ones who know they need me."

There will always be cranky religious people around who wonder why Jesus showed up to hang out with you. Ignore them. They think they have it all figured out. But here's a warning. If you think you have it all figured out–you're one of the cranky religious people.

People who assume they have it all figured out aren't fun to be around. They look down on the rest of us because we know we're still working it out. They like to make you feel like you're irredeemable, but Jesus says – you are redeemed. The religious folks will treat you like a discarded sinner, but Jesus calls you son or daughter. Religious people will keep telling you that you are lost, while Jesus simply says, "follow me." Religious folks will show up with a list of all their qualifying expectations. Jesus will invite you into a lifetime of figuring it out with him.

FOR NOW

When we start talking about all the cool things Jesus did, it gets easy to focus on the cross, the resurrection, and our beliefs about what happens after we die. I believe in all of those things but don't miss this. Jesus speaks the words "follow me" over all of our lives because Jesus wants to be with you right now. You don't have to wait until everything is a train wreck to experience the good news of Jesus. Yes! Jesus will redeem your worst day. But you can experience the goodness of following Jesus through life here and now!

Matthew became convinced of that by what he saw. He saw things that were so incredible he had to write them down! If you saw something unexplainable happen, what would you do? You'd probably put it on your Instagram or make a video about it for social media. We can't ignore that bad things happen all the time, but we all see pretty amazing stuff happen everyday, too. Don't ignore the incredible things because you're too busy worrying about the bad stuff. Don't overlook everyday miracles because you're worried about wading through the mud.

Please hear me. Bad stuff happens every day, too. Jesus never promised bad things would stop. He promised us a path through them with him. Wading through the hard stuff is different when you're with Jesus. I'm convinced Matthew wrote his Gospel story because being with Jesus everyday taught him that following Jesus wasn't about what happens after you die. Following Jesus is about a better way to live.

CHAPTER 4
WRONG TURNS

DIRECTIONS

"Yeah, can I be in your TV show?" That was the phone call my brother decided to make one day. No kidding. He picked up the phone and cold-called a talent agency in North Carolina after learning they were in charge of casting for his favorite show.

In the days before social media, video meetings, and YouTube, we had to learn about stuff through an ancient device called a telephone. One day Brian decided he would reach out and see what might happen.

When my brother called the talent agency, I'm not sure what he expected, but he was surprised by the response. The agency told him to send them a picture. Which makes sense. They were in charge of finding people to be in a show about a lot of attractive teenagers. They didn't want someone like me showing up on set someday. If you had chipped teeth from too many soccer balls to the face and a nose you could see coming around the corner, you probably weren't getting in. But well, if you looked like my brother, you were in. He got in.

After spending his spring break hanging out on set filming, he returned home full of big dreams. He finished the semester at the university, dropped out of school, and packed up his stuff to move to the east coast.

The day he left, we loaded all his stuff into a couple of cars and hit the road. Man, that was a long day. Back then, we didn't have the voice of a little robot Irish lady in our iPhone telling us what turns to take. So, we used an ancient device called a map.

We drove all day. We drove all night. We drove through the Smokey Mountains and just kept driving. We stopped too long for lunch. We took in too many sights on the way. We didn't get in much of a hurry. Finally, it was so late that we realized it was time to stop and sleep.

Back then, when you were on a road trip, you couldn't find little private rooms or old homes someone had decided to rent out through an app on the internet. You had to stay in these ancient accommodations called hotels. The upside is that they were everywhere. So we decided to stop at one. It was full. We stopped at another hotel. It was full. So was the next one. And the next one. Apparently, they were all full. There was no room at the inn. It was starting to feel like a Christmas story.

We decided to put some more miles behind us and banked on finding one a little closer to our final stop. So we took off back down the road. My brother was driving while I watched a movie on a portable DVD player. I was trying to be good company by staying awake. Then it happened.

I looked up and saw a sign we weren't supposed to see on our trip, "WELCOME TO VIRGINIA." Oh boy. We had driven in the wrong direction.

WRONG TURNS

We have all found ourselves in a similar situation. We got lost. We took a wrong turn somewhere. We wound up where we never intended to go. It happens. I've learned that Jesus doesn't get mad at us for missing the turn. Instead, he shows up to help us find our way.

People will get mad at you when you miss their expectations. You may get mad at yourself for missing a turn from time to time. Some people build their entire careers, or even their lives, around celebrating missed turns.

When you do miss it, there are consequences. Sometimes, there are logical consequences, like winding up somewhere you never meant to go. We hadn't planned on going to Virginia. No one plans to be an addict, to suffer a devastating divorce, or find themselves crippled emotionally because of a lifetime of wrong turns.

That's the danger of wrong turns. If we don't start moving in the right direction, we'll keep making wrong turns. They add up over time.

One of the movies I watched with my brother on our wayward road trip was literally called *Wrong Turn*. Ironic. It's a terrible movie about crazy cannibal hillbillies–in Virginia. None of the hillbillies I know are cannibals. And none of them live in Virginia. But the premise is pretty on point as metaphors go: wrong turns can lead to bad things.

Taking a wrong turn on a road trip can land you in the middle of some unexpected surroundings, but so will taking a wrong turn with your life. You'll eventually find yourself in unfamiliar territory. It's important for us to realize this isn't just something that happens on the outside. I'm not just talking about rooms and environments here.

When you make wrong turns a habit, you eventually wind up in a place you never wanted to be. You become a stranger to yourself. You wake up one day wondering why you think the way you do. And you may not even like the person looking back in your mirror.

This is another reason why everyday with Jesus is better than any day without him. When you reach a fork in the road, you learn to take the right direction. It starts by asking Jesus which way he would go.

WWJD

In high school it was trendy to run around wearing bracelets with "What would Jesus do?" written on them. It was like a low-tech Fitbit for your soul. Instead of being there to remind you how many steps you'd taken, it was supposed to remind you to take the next step toward Jesus. We should all be trying to figure out what Jesus would do. Once you realize Jesus actually likes you and wants to be with you, it makes figuring out what he would do a little easier.

The truth is simple, but it takes work. When figuring out what Jesus would do–we make it way too complicated. But Jesus told us how to figure it out. Jesus said things like follow my voice, serve others, love your neighbor, be holy, and love God.

When my brother and I were on our trip, we needed our map. Every turn mattered when it came to getting to our final destination. Most Christians I've known have been focused on talking a lot about our final destination. Awesome. I'm 100% a fan of Heaven and, equally, of trying to get as many people there as we can. Still, we should take care not to treat every moment and every decision like something that could hijack the end result.

I think Jesus talked so much about following him because he wanted to show us the way. Yes, the final destination is a big deal. I like the part in the Bible about eternity with a God who deeply loves us and everyone's tears getting wiped away. But life with Jesus is about way more than what happens when you die.

Wait a second?! There's more than heaven? Yeah, I know. It's crazy.

Jesus showed us the way. He wants us to follow him. "What would Jesus do?" becomes our guiding philosophy because we all need a guide. We all need to understand where we want to go. We all need to know how to get there. We all need to know how to make the next right choice.

We eventually got my brother to his new apartment on the coast. We spent a week helping him settle in and taking in a new city. It was a fun week. But the thing that has always stuck with me about that trip is the trip itself. It's one of the only times in my adult life I've taken off across the country with nothing but a map. The map was the key to arriving at the right place.

Jesus' words to his friends were their map. When he said to them something like, "Go and make disciples in your city, and your country, and the whole world," He wasn't being generic. He was giving them specific directions. He was offering a route they could follow with their lives. And they did it.

The beautiful thing about life with Jesus is that it is life with Jesus. The end result sounds pretty awesome, but the road trip is pretty awesome, too. Because it is *with* Jesus.

When we take the trip with Jesus, we learn what Jesus wants. We can better answer what he would do. A lot of people are really good at looking like they follow

Jesus. They say and appear to do all of the right things. But their heart is a mess. It's full of wrong turns.

Jesus talked about people like this. He said, "They look like they're doing it right, but their hearts are far from me."

When we begin to spend everyday with Jesus, we'll stop looking like we're doing it right, and start to actually do it right. Because we won't be concerned about appearances. We'll stop caring what anyone thinks about our next turn. We'll only have eyes and ears for one set of directions, "What would Jesus do?" As we do, we'll stop following Jesus for the prize and start following Jesus with our heart.

Living with Jesus everyday means we call timeout on lip service. We give up on faking it till we make it. We trade in a life of appearing to follow Jesus for a life of actually following Jesus. The end result will be pretty awesome, but everyday with Jesus is pretty awesome, too.

CHAPTER 5
SATISFIED

FATIGUE

During the COVID-19 pandemic, I hit a metaphorical wall. I didn't know where to go or what to do to help the people in my life. Imagine running around with a bucket on your head, and you have the right idea. It wasn't just any wall; the wall I hit was like one of those walls in an escape room where you can't find the door, and you're pretty sure the clock's running faster than it should. The pandemic seemed to multiply problems like Gremlins at a waterpark. I was swamped! A few weeks in, I was as exhausted as someone trying to explain TikTok to their grandparents.

I knew I couldn't keep it up, so I dialed my buddy Kevin because he has a big heart, a brilliant mind, and slings loving wisdom around him in heaps. Kevin is unique because he is both a pastor and a licensed therapist. He's like a superhero who can straddle the complicated boundaries between emotional, mental, and spiritual well-being. Kevin's also the type of guy who can find the silver lining in a lint bag. To my surprise, he diagnosed me with something called "compassion fatigue." It sounded like a side effect they'd sneak in at the end of a medicine commercial. His pro tip? "Bro, pack a bag and get yourself to an island." Killer advice! I'd be building sand castles in no time! If only the airports had gotten the memo. They were all closed.

My wife came up with a great solution. We packed a few bags, dropped our kids off with her sister, and found a quiet hotel in a city not so far away. All we did for a few days was rest, take walks, and spend time together. It was long overdue.

Everyone has a profound need for rest. Not just a nap. Or catching eight hours every night between their sheets. Rest. Letting everything drop for a chance to recharge and rejuvenate.

There was a similar moment in the gospels. Jesus' disciples had been out preaching and teaching all over the countryside. They come back to Jesus with bags under their eyes, looking disheveled. Jesus noticed they looked like they'd just binged three seasons of *The Chosen* without a break. So he called a time out for some rest and recovery. Jesus knew they were zapped. He knew what they needed to do. His suggestion was for them to all get away and rest.

Jesus and the disciples got in the boat and went to a remote place by themselves. Apparently, someone saw them leave, and word got out. From the surrounding towns, people went out on foot, running, and got there ahead of them. Have you ever had to take a work call on vacation? This moment for the disciples was a bit like that, only instead of solving one problem–about 5,000 people showed up. People who ran to be where Jesus was going to be. No one reading this will get up next Sunday and run to church, except maybe your crazy friend who runs marathons in his sleep. The people in this story ran to Jesus. They *ran!*

CROWD CONTROL

The crowds in the Gospel story ran to Jesus for one simple reason. He had a reputation for meeting needs. People around Jesus had begun to intuitively know what Jesus hopes all of us will learn to bank on. Jesus satisfies the deepest needs of our hearts. He satisfies on all levels.

Jesus arrived on the scene with his friends to find a huge crowd waiting. I would have probably decided to keep sailing. Not Jesus. His heart was moved at the sight of all the people who had run to be near him. So, instead of taking the day off–he started teaching them. This is how I know I will never be as kind as Jesus. Because if you showed up in the middle of my vacation, compassion isn't the first thing I'm going to think of. But Jesus loved the crowd.

Fast forward, and the disciples started playing the role of every employee at 4:55 PM on a Friday. "Can we wrap this up, Jesus?" They were checking their watches and probably had restaurant apps open, scouting dinner spots. Essentially, Peter and the boys said, "Give an altar call, and let's get some dinner.

I get it. The story even tells us at the beginning that the disciples hadn't even had time to eat. They were hangry! Then Jesus did something they probably should have seen coming. He asked them to do for others what they hadn't done for themselves. Jesus said, "We're not sending these people away. You fix supper for them." Jesus told them to solve the problem. This is a good reminder. Anytime you point out a problem to God, there are always three fingers pointing back at you.

This happens to me way too often. I want to send someone on their way so God can fix their issue. And God is saying, "I sent them to you."

Have you ever had a "you do it" moment with God? We all probably have. Did you respond like the disciples did? They replied, "Are you serious? You want us to spend a fortune on food for their supper?" Jesus didn't tell them to throw a heap of money at the problem. He told them to find the people some food.

I love that they thought he was messing with them. This is a great insight into Jesus' sense of humor. Jesus knew they didn't have the resources to feed these people. Jesus knew they needed his help, but he wanted them to be part of it. Jesus routinely asks us to participate in something beyond our means—because he is our means. What does that even mean? It *means* Jesus loves for his friends to join in his work. We don't do it. We witness it!

NEED

"How many loaves of bread do you have?" Jesus asked. Their impromptu inventory didn't take long. They were down to five Cracker Barrel biscuits and a couple of cans of tuna.

Jesus got them all to sit down in groups of fifty or a hundred—they probably looked like a patchwork quilt of wildflowers spread across the surroundings. If you've ever been to an outside concert where everyone was shouting for the encore–I can't help but think that's what this moment with Jesus looked like!

It was a huge crowd of hungry people! But they came to Jesus hungry for more than food. They didn't know it yet, but they were about to leave, satisfied by something most of them would never know how to describe. Only Jesus satisfies like that. What he did next was amazing.

Jesus took the five loaves and two fish and lifted his face to heaven in prayer. He blessed, broke, and gave the bread to his friends, and the disciples in turn gave it to all the people who had gathered around. But Jesus wasn't finished. He did the same with the fish.

Have you ever wondered what Jesus prayed in this story? We don't know. This wasn't "God is good, God is great, we are thankful for this food, Amen," or "Rubadubdub, thanks for the grub, let's eat."

It's remarkable that later, when Peter was telling the story to some friends, he couldn't remember what Jesus prayed. He was so hungry he didn't recall the single greatest dinner prayer in all of history. Instead of remembering what Jesus said, Peter and the boys remembered what Jesus did.

What did Jesus do? Jesus blessed the meal. What do you need Jesus to bless in your life? Where have you been coming up empty lately? Jesus might not give you what you want. But I'm convinced he'll give you what you really need.

There's been plenty of times I thought I wanted one thing. But God gave me something else. Guess which one was better for me in the long run? It's happened more times than I can remember. I'm trying to remember that what I need is always better than what I want.

Jesus broke the meal, too. Jesus probably could have fed the crowd without breaking any of the bread, but that's not how it happened. He didn't feed the people without breaking some stuff. Sometimes, we're so busy hoping God will keep us whole. But maybe he really just wants us to have what we need. Sometimes, something needs to break first.

I've lived through enough broken promises to learn what trust really looks like. I've lived through some broken dreams, too, and learned what hope *really* is. I've wandered through enough broken moments in life to discover what real peace is. Pain sucks, but sometimes it's just the teacher we need. Everyday I have bumped into a difficult moment. Jesus was there. Sometimes, Jesus will break what we bring to make what we need.

Jesus could have fed the people on his own. When you're the one who invented the bread, you don't need anyone's help making more. Jesus didn't roll that way. That's why the guys didn't remember the words Jesus said. They were too busy focusing on what Jesus did. He involved his friends.

When you look at the stories about Jesus, it's a repeating theme. Jesus often asked his friends to be part of his work. And he does the same with you and I. Especially on any day that ends in "y".

Think about this. Jesus gave the crowd the meal. But *who* did he give it to? He gave it to his friends. Jesus had the disciples give the food to the crowd.

Jesus has to bless it. Jesus has to break it. But he wants you to be the one to give it.

He does the blessing when blessing is needed. He does the breaking if breaking is needed. Jesus gives first. We just give away what he gave us. God's economy is crazy cool. Do you know what happened next?

The story says they all ate until they were full. Everyone ate all they needed. It was the best fish fry ever. The disciples finally got to eat in spectacular fashion, and so did everyone else!

Jesus gave the people what they needed. All of the people. He gave the crowd insight and encouragement. He gave them help and hope. But he gave the disciples some stuff, too. Namely, Jesus gave them a chance to get off the bench and get into the game. They had to move past how tired they were–and fully rely on him. And when they did–everyone ate their fill.

No one was left out. Everyone who showed up that day left satisfied. The crowd was satisfied. The disciples were satisfied. Jesus was satisfied. That's a pretty great day.

REALLY SATISFIED

So many people spend their lives spinning their wheels in pursuit of possessions, achievements, or relationships. None of those things are bad. They just aren't Jesus. True satisfaction comes when you're walking everyday with him.

The disciples gathered twelve baskets of leftovers even though more than five thousand people were there. Do you know what I find remarkable? Why did the people have baskets with them? They thought about bringing a basket but didn't pack dinner? Or maybe they just came expecting Jesus to do something remarkable. Everyday I want to come expecting Jesus to do something.

Why was this story important? What was at stake for these people? Their life. Their religious identity, which also included their cultural and national identity. They were facing a major crisis of faith, identity, and purpose.

What happened? They all ate and were satisfied. The

people followed Jesus into the wild to hear the truth. Why? Because they had become so disheartened by the religious pretenders, they were forced to depend on.

Think about what was at stake for them. A lot. Financial. Social. Emotional. Spiritual. Jesus satisfied all of those things. Not because he gave them what they wanted but because he gave them what they needed.

Who are you in this story? Are you the crowd or the disciples? The crowd ran to Jesus. There are times when we must run to Jesus. The disciples rested with Jesus. There are seasons when we must be at rest. Both were satisfied.

The other day, my boys were playing together. You know how kids are when they just can't seem to get along. But they were doing well. They were being kind. Having fun. And then one of them screamed out, "I am not satisfied!" Well, we've all been there, haven't we?

When was the last time you thought that? *I'm not satisfied.* There's a lot about life we could be dissatisfied with. I don't know your circumstances, but I know mine. Life is just hard sometimes. We could all list a lot of struggles.

What happens when we are satisfied with the wrong things? When we are satisfied with the wrong things, eventually we will no longer be satisfied. "Nate, that's common sense." Yeah, but let's take a moment to acknowledge how this plays out.

Sometimes, we pursue an arbitrary sense of happiness. Sometimes, we chase stuff. We think temporary things can bring us eternal happiness. When we are satisfied with the wrong thing for too long. We usually hit a wall. And find out the truth the hard way. And then we wonder what in the world life is really even about. It leaves us cut off at the knees. It leaves us directionless and without purpose. No one is more miserable than someone without purpose because what you aim your life at is where you go. When we live satisfied with the wrong things, we are just kind of existing. At its best, life like that is dull. At its worst, it's an empty existence.

We are meant to be satisfied in Christ. Real contentment is found with Jesus. Real purpose is discovered with Jesus. Real fulfillment comes from living life with Jesus.

Jesus offered the gathered crowd real satisfaction. Ignore him, and they live as usual. They were already fed up with that. They had gone into the wild to find satisfaction. They went to the wild to find hope. They found Jesus.

You and I are living through wild times. Think about the anger. The craziness of the day. The prevailing sense of unrest, emotional outrage, and social dissatisfaction. We need something to happen.

We need a moment with Jesus. The disciples needed a moment with Jesus. The crowd needed a moment with Jesus. They all ate their fill. They all left satisfied.

Only Jesus satisfies. What do we do with that? Simple. We come to Jesus everyday.

Dissatisfied? Come to Jesus. Materialism left you empty? Come to Jesus. Outrage left you empty? Come to Jesus. Work left you empty? Come to Jesus. Family left you empty? Come to Jesus.

The crowd came to Jesus with empty baskets. Some of them took home leftovers. What does that mean for us? When you're empty, bring it to Jesus. He is more than enough.

My Uncle David and Aunt JoAnn were some of my heroes. They lived satisfied with Jesus. A couple of weeks before she passed away, Aunt JoAnn was at the store. She stepped into the checkout line, smiling as usual. A young man in front of her turned and said, "Ma'am, I like your smile so much I would like to buy your groceries."

Aunt JoAnn replied, "Son, I'm smiling like this because I have Jesus in my heart." Uncle David and Aunt JoAnn lived full of satisfaction. The kind that only comes from Jesus.

We all need to ask an important question. What keeps me from being satisfied? What is keeping me from enjoying contentment? What holds me back from living life with the joy of the Lord tattooed to my face for everyone to see and experience? When we figure out the answer to that question, we need to do all we can to change it!

For some of u,s that will be a subtle shift. For others, it may take drastic changes. But here is the litmus test. If what you're holding onto is leaving you empty–it ain't Jesus.

Jesus blesses. Jesus breaks. Jesus gives. Jesus satisfies.

The Psalmist wrote, "Taste and see that the Lord is good." What will happen as we lean into the satisfaction that only Jesus brings into our lives? We will stop chasing stuff. We will stop pursuing arbitrary notions of happiness. We'll stop moving through life like someone with a bucket over his head. Instead, we'll be anchored in peace, goodness, kindness, and self-control.

A few months ago, I sat by my Uncle David's bedside. My family had called me in because he was about to go home to heaven. He had pastored the same church from 1973 until 2020. 47 years!

He was such an incredible example of living life satisfied in Christ alone. I read the bible to him that afternoon for hours. We sang hymns and prayed.

He couldn't speak very well, but he was whispering scripture. He couldn't stand up, but he kept lifting his right hand in worship. When my cousin tried to get him to eat a little food, I heard him clear as a bell, say, "I'll fill my belly with the Word of God." That's what living satisfied in Christ looks like.

We don't have to wait until our final moments to experience our best moments. Any day is a good day to start. Today sounds like the perfect day. If you've never taken that step, what are you waiting for? Those who have done it won't be empty. We'll be full. Full of the joy of the Lord. Full of the Spirit of God. Full of Love for our neighbor. If we show up to Jesus fatigued, empty, and expecting, we can leave with exactly what we need.

CHAPTER 6
THE COST

YOU'RE INVITED

Do you ever stop and think about what's next in your life? Perhaps you've sat down at some point in the summer and wondered, "How can I finish this year well?" Or if you're like most people, you come at it sometime around New Year's thinking, "How can this year be a great one."

Here's how. Live for Jesus everyday. Why? Because everyday with Jesus is better than any day without him. But I'll be the first to admit we've made living for Jesus a lot more complicated than it actually is.

Living for Jesus changes your life. It will make you stronger than you ever thought you could be. You will increase in wisdom in ways you never before imagined. You will have peace in your life that seemed impossible only a week ago.

Living for Jesus everyday means inviting his

strength into your everyday life. It means inviting his love to your table daily. What could be stronger than learning straight from Jesus?

I want everyone I meet to embrace a life spent following Jesus. We learn to follow him with our hearts, our minds, our soul, and our strength. I don't want to be kind of devoted to Jesus. I don't want to take a half-measured approach to living with Jesus. I want to go *all in*. I want you to as well. I want it for my kids, my friends, and my family. Jesus wants it for you way more than I do. He wants us to be fully devoted to every step with him.

WHAT DOES IT MEAN?

Commonly, those following Jesus are referred to as Christians. Maybe you've occasionally heard them called "Christ-followers." Both are references to people who are supposed to be trying to live everyday with Jesus.

There's another old word people like to use a lot when they talk about living everyday for Jesus. It's the word *disciple*. What is a disciple? A disciple is someone who learns. A disciple is someone who follows someone else. A disciple of Jesus is someone who follows Jesus. Why? In order to become like Jesus.

In our society, when we learn something, we take a class. We sit in rows with other people, or we watch a seminar over the internet. We listen to someone talk about their subject, and then we take a test to prove we learned it. That's not what Jesus had in mind for his disciples.

The truth is we are all being discipled by someone. We are "learning" from someone. We learn from family, teachers, peers, music, and movies. Someone has taught you how to live. Someone taught you how to think. You learned how to make life decisions. You learned how to use TikTok, your coffee maker, and even a toothbrush. You have learned everything you know.

If you call yourself a Christian, then you are calling yourself a disciple of Jesus. You are stating you presume to live everyday with Jesus. His heart for you is to learn how to live life with him, but it's not like starting kindergarten and then graduating to Heaven. Jesus has invited you to follow Him, so you can invite others to follow him, too.

Jesus made it clear to his friends what following him meant. Jesus had been traveling the countryside. He preached in small towns. He healed people in droves. He fed thousands. He taught in their gathering places and amassed followers. He cast out demons and raised dead people to life. He did amazing things that drew massive crowds.

And then he started making his way to Jerusalem, where his public life would culminate in his murder. He was murdered by the religious elite on the cross, and he knew it was coming. He even told his disciples it was about to happen. But they didn't understand. And then he said something that probably surprised them, "If anyone wants to follow me, he has to deny himself, pick up his cross everyday, and follow me."

This was a clear invitation that probably left them wondering what was going to happen next? By this point, Jesus had crowds trying to follow him everywhere. They wanted to see miracles and experience wonders. They had never heard or seen anyone like Jesus. They were used to upright religious prudes who were more interested in rules than the grace and goodness of God—and then came Jesus. They flocked to him. So he wanted to make sure he was clear. Everyone was invited. But the invitation was not easy.

Many were in it for the spectacle. As long as it seemed advantageous, they wanted to follow Jesus. So Jesus stopped to clear the air about what it actually took to follow him. He wanted them to understand what it meant to be his disciple.

"If you're coming with me, be ready to put down selfishness and carry your own cross." This was his conditional statement.

It's like Jesus was laying it out for them, "If you're daring enough to follow me. If you're brave enough to follow me. If you're weak and you need real help. If you're lost, and you need real change." Anyone can come to Jesus. But—if we actually want to follow Jesus, we will follow where is going.

WHERE TO?

Where was Jesus going? He had "set his face toward Jerusalem." He was marching toward the fulfillment of his mission. It would culminate in his death and resurrection. He wanted his friends to understand how steep the price was for their next steps. Denying yourself is no small thing.

How do we deny ourselves? We don't do it by giving in to every whim, living selfish lives, or choosing our own interests. We do it by delaying gratification, rejecting selfishness, and choosing others. That's what carrying your cross through life looks like. That's what it means to live for Jesus everyday.

Often, this verse is taught to mean that Jesus was saying following him is all about sacrifice. Maybe he did mean it that way. But let me point out something important. Jesus was the only one sacrificed. He did it so you and I wouldn't have to. Because he was the only one Holy enough to pull it off.

When Jesus said, "Take up your cross," everyone listening instantly thought of something way different than you or I think. We think of an icon of faith. Sometimes, people will kiss a cross on a necklace. Or we think of Easter and the sacrifice Jesus made. That's not what the cross meant to anyone in that moment when Jesus said it.

The cross was a symbol of incredible shame. It was a curse. Jesus said this before he experienced the cross in the way we have come to see it. Was Jesus asking us to carry shame everyday? No, and yes. Let me explain.

No. Jesus does not want you to live under constant shame. That would be both belittling and emotionally destructive. There is a difference between living in shame and being ashamed.

A person who lives under the weight of shame is crushed. They are apprehensive, unconfident, distracted, and doubtful. Their life is bound up by all of that, and there's usually not a lot of joy. No good father wants that for his kids. God does not want it for you.

So what was Jesus saying? Because he definitely said, "Take up your cross". The cross was terrible *because* it exposed shame. The shame of the one who hung on it. The accused literally hung there naked with a sign over their head declaring their crime.

For us to take up our cross, we have to acknowledge our sin. We have to admit how we were wrong. Taking up our cross is about admitting responsibility for our actions.

We don't see this very often anymore. In fact, we see the opposite. People do something crazy and dare others to think it's shameful. If we take responsibility for our actions, it highlights the amazing thing Jesus did on his cross.

Our cross is about our shame. Jesus' cross is also about our shame. Because he had nothing to be ashamed of.

They were traveling to Jerusalem as they had this discussion. It's likely they were using one of the

Roman-built roads. A road that just a few years earlier had been the site of hundreds of simultaneous crucifixions during a rebellion. It's even possible that, as Jesus said, "take up your cross," those listening could still see the remains of dozens of crosses on the side of the road.

Jesus was saying, "Acknowledge your guilt". To his friends, he was saying remember. Remember what you've done and how you've messed up.

He wants us to acknowledge and to remember our mistakes. He wants to be aware that our sin is our rebellion against God. But not so we will feel perpetually guilty. Jesus wants us to remember how we got it wrong so we will remember how he made it right.

EVERYDAY INVITATION

Being a follower of Jesus is not a one-time prayer or moment. It's not like we pray a prayer once, and then we're good to go for the rest of our lives. Following Jesus is a daily pursuit. Every day we acknowledge what we have done. Every day, we accept what Jesus did for us. Every day, we embrace the next right thing. It's about the choices and decisions that add up to a lifetime of following Jesus. Every day, we take note of our place in His Kingdom.

The love Jesus has for you calls to you from across history. It reaches out to you across time and space. He beckons you and I to follow him.

It's about being like Jesus. Learning from Jesus. Moving through this life the way Jesus would and did.

Jesus extends his invitation. It is the invitation Jesus wants for you. It is the invitation he wants you to share with others. It is an invitation you accept all over again every day.

Sometimes we think we are following Jesus, but in reality, we have invited Jesus to follow us. Like we're asking him to approve our endeavors. And there's nothing wrong with asking him to bless you, but if that's your entire faith, it's an upside down relationship.

Like saying, "Jesus I don't want to follow where you're going, but you can ride shotgun and keep me safe. And maybe hand me snacks every once in a while." That would make for a bad song and an even worse way to live.

You will not wake up one day and go, "I'm *all in* for Jesus." That's not how it works. It's very intentional. It's a personal decision. God draws us to him with his love and grace. But he doesn't force himself on us. We have to make choices to learn, follow, and obey God.

We were at some friends' house a few months ago. My buddy Nick had just fixed up his pool, but it was a little cold for me. I'm a total pansy when it comes to cold.

What did my kids do? They just all jumped right in. I knew jumping in would be best, but I didn't want to take the plunge. So I tried to tiptoe into the shallow end. It was so much worse!

No one can jump in for you. You have to jump. You

have to take the plunge. You have to go all in. You have to take up your cross daily.

No one can make you a disciple. Ultimately, you can't rely on your parent's faith. You can't rely on your religious upbringing. You can't rely on a favorite preacher. You can't give excuses or have a victim mentality. You have to be intentional. Nothing worth anything happens by accident.

I have to be intentional with my marriage. Jamie is amazing. We've been married for sixteen years. We have four wonderful children. We are committed to one another. We are in love with one another. We are loyal to one another. Many good things come naturally in our marriage. But we have to be more intentional about some things because of the rigorous schedule we keep and the demands of raising a young family. We have to be intentional about going on dates and affirming one another. It doesn't happen as much as either of us would like.

It takes intentional decisions to take up your cross. We aren't going to live everyday with Jesus by accident. We won't spend time with scripture by accident. We don't grow and change by accident. We don't develop life-giving, deep friendships by accident.

Following Jesus is committing to a lifestyle of growing. Growing to become more like Christ. Daily choices, and moment-to-moment decisions add up to a lifetime of following and service.

CHAPTER 7
THE BETTER SAVIOR

ON THE ROCKS

My friends surprised me one day with a party. But not just any party. A bachelor party, because I was getting married.

We did a marathon paintball session on a tactical training course. We ate like kings. And then we all went swimming at our favorite local water hole. That's when things got really interesting.

On the far side of the wide creek loomed two massive boulders. They sat there like ancient watchers having observed the masses for as long as people had been coming to this creek. It was common practice for people to scale the cleft between the boulders to reach the top. And what did you do from the top? You jumped off of course.

Me and my buddies had made the trip and were goofing off on top of the rocks when one of my best friends decided to make the trip across in order to join us on the rocks. But there was a catch. He couldn't really swim. He could sort of paddle across, and he did—almost.

When he had made it a little more than halfway—right as he reached the deepest part—he started to panic. Under he went. We all stared in disbelief, shocked into momentary inaction.

But this was my friend. Someone important to me. I had known him since boyhood. He was like a brother to me. There was no way I was going to just watch. So I dove in after him.

I was to him in a split second. He was in full panic mode, arms thrashing as he struggled to keep his head above water. I did the only thing I could to save him. I came up behind him and wrapped him in a headlock. I literally squeezed the air out of him in order to drag him to safety. I hauled him to the beach struggling the whole way, until we arrived where he was able to breathe in safety again.

I have saved a few people in the water in my life. Not because I'm good at it. But because I was in the right place at the right time. And I wasn't afraid to try. But I'm no savior. None of us are.

Jesus is our savior. He sees when we swim out beyond our depth. And he's just waiting for us to acknowledge how much we need him.

This happens to me all of the time. I find myself over my head in my commitments, or in my bad attitude. I take on more than I should. Or I reject wisdom in some reckless pursuit. The results are rarely pretty. Thankfully, Jamie is usually there to remind me how I messed up in her loving way.

That's when I acknowledge my trouble. It's when I call out for help. Jesus wants to rescue each of us, but he isn't watching to see what makes us feel good. He's trying to help us keep our heads above the water.

Once we ask for help he isn't going to consider our permission, our feelings, or our wishes. He will move us away from whatever kills us in order to get us back on our feet.

From his perspective he sees better than we do. He knows us better than our friends do. And he doesn't freeze up when things get dramatic. Instead he is waiting on pins and needles for the chance to charge forward and snag you from the clutches of disaster.

It reflects what he did in the grave. Jesus died for us. But he didn't stay dead. He charged the gates of hell. He took death's victory away, forever.

FANFARE

People cheered and clapped as I hauled my friend out of the water. I sat down exhausted. I heard the fanfare around me, but I was really just thankful my friend was okay.

What happened over the next few weeks was a mixture of funny, awesome and a bit weird. My friend kept showing up at my apartment with my favorite coffee. I was grateful at first. Who doesn't like free coffee?

Then it clicked for me one day. My friend was bringing me coffee because he thought he owed me something. Dropping $100 in a month on coffee was the only way he knew to express his appreciation for what I had done.

But there was a problem. I didn't save my friend because I was hoping for something in return. I didn't haul him to safety secretly wishing he would start bringing me an iced caramel macchiato everyday. I saved my friend because I love him.

Hearing someone say "thank you" is cool. Hearing it everyday for something that happened a long time ago gets weird. So I asked him to stop.

There's a big difference between me jumping off a rock for a buddy and Jesus jumping out of Heaven for everyone's buddy. I did it for someone I love. So did he. I know my friend was grateful for my actions but I didn't need him to make a big deal out of it.

Jesus doesn't need our constant fanfare either. He isn't insecure about what happened on the cross. He isn't insecure about throwing down with death and coming out the victor. He doesn't need anything from us. He never will. But that's not the point.

He rescued you and I from our sin because he loves us. He really does love you. He loves you so much he interrupted human history in order to turn the tide.

The victory of Jesus belongs to him. But he shared it with you and me. Not in the sense that we had anything to do with it. But because he loves us. We get to participate in his victory. Not because we are victorious, but because he is. Not because we are good, but because he is. Not because we are holy, but because he is.

Sometimes when I look around at the answers people keep coming up with for all of the problems we face it makes me think of that day at the creek. People are out there way over their head. They are drowning. They need a savior. But they don't see it.

Way too many people see themselves as the way to save themselves. It's not a new idea, but it's a pretty pervasive one these days. It's not going to work. It never has.

We need a better savior. We need Jesus. We need him everyday.

EVERYDAY GRATITUDE

The coffee from my friend seemed weird after a while so I asked him to stop. Not because I wasn't thankful. Not because I doubted his gratitude. Not because I don't like coffee. I asked him to stop because it was unnecessary.

These days my friend comes over a few times every month to play board games with my family. Because we are competitive and opinionated, those nights can be intense. If my friend and I are arguing, do you know what I don't do? I don't say, "Hey, remember that time I saved your life?" I don't wield the reminder of what I did as a method for getting my way.

In my conversations with people it seems more and more often that people get confused about Jesus' motivations. As if he died on a cross for us so we would spend the rest of eternity saying "thanks" on a cosmic scale. Jesus is the son of God. If a "thank you" was all he was after you and I both know he could have found a way to get it without dying an excruciating death on the cross.

Jesus doesn't need our gratitude. He doesn't need anything from us. He also doesn't need our worship. I realize that statement will make some people nervous. And this next one will make many really uncomfortable. He doesn't need us to gather with our friends in a building every Sunday morning and sing some songs. Even if the songs are beautiful and lovely. Jesus doesn't need it.

What I learned from my friend and the incident at the creek taught me a lot about Jesus. I didn't need him to bring me coffee everyday. It was unnecessary. Why? Because he is my friend. But he needed a way to say thank you.

Do you know how we fixed the tension between what I didn't need and what he did need? We didn't. We didn't change anything because there was nothing to change. I told him he didn't have to bring me coffee. I told him I knew he was grateful. I told him I was glad he was okay. I told him I was thankful he was like a brother to me. He still is. We were texting about his new job last night. Why? Because he is my friend.

Jesus doesn't need you to put your gratitude on an endless loop. But you don't need to stop being grateful either. It's not either/or. It's both/and. You and I need a savior. Not the kind of savior our culture tries to shove into the spotlight. Not a political figure. Not a pop culture hero. We need a better savior. We need Jesus, and we need him everyday.

CHAPTER 8
UP A HILL

SAGES AND SAINTS

One of the things I love the most about my friend Greg is that he is not a flashy guy. Well, unless you've ever seen him do a wheelie on a dirt bike. He gets up early everyday and puts one foot in front of another as he follows Jesus. Greg learned a long time ago that everyday with Jesus is better than any day without him. His daily life takes him to some extraordinary places. Most of them are the kinds of places where cell phones don't work and four wheel drive is required.

When he first moved to Guatemala decades ago, he didn't speak Spanish, and all he had for transportation was a dirt bike. After finding someone who spoke a little English, and could explain the difference between "hello" and "hungry", Greg began to translate his sermons into the native language. He would travel into the mountains, and once a crowd had gathered to see what the strange gringo was up to he would read his sermons to them.

It wasn't easy. At all. But Greg learned a long time ago that everyday with Jesus is better than any day without him. He knew it because he had spent quite a few days without Jesus. Once Greg was introduced to Jesus he refused to go another day without him. For Greg that means going where Jesus leads.

Greg gets up everyday and sets about following Jesus. He's always ready to take the next step. Those steps have taken him on the adventure of a lifetime. One I've been privileged to participate in on occasion.

Greg has waited out night time storms beneath trees in the middle of mudslides praying. He has overcome physical attacks from deranged people. He has walked more miles than most of us could begin to imagine across terrain you won't find anywhere in a local zip code.

My friend's first village to call home was a quaint place called Lampacoy. Like so many of the tiny villages in the area, it sets high in the mountains. When Greg first moved to the area an elderly couple adopted him and he would stay with them for months at a time.

On one trip to Guatemala Greg took me to Lampacoy. There I got to meet the elderly widow who had become a mother to my friend. I sat in her tiny room made of mud plastered walls next to the one simple table where her well-worn bible lay open from near constant use.

I was moved by the focused faith of a lady who clearly meant so much to someone who meant so much to me. There in the small room of a simple woman high in the mountains of a remote village was a tiny lady who stood tall in her faith. She could barely walk but her journey was a decades long story of everyday steps with Jesus. Greg was the guy who moved to Guatemala because Jesus told him too, but here was the lady with an everyday faith that encouraged Greg.

On my next trip to Guatemala I brought Jamie. We crammed a lot into a week with my friend, but I knew we had to take my wife to Lampacoy. There Greg took her to meet the saintly widow of the mountain village. My wife would tell you with great zeal that it was her favorite day on our trip. She keeps a picture of the precious woman in her office to remember the moment.

THE PATH TO GRATITUDE

In the movies there is always a moment when the desperate traveler goes in search of the secret to life or some miracle to solve his problem. It always takes the hero of the story to the one with all the answers. In my attempts to do the same I've wound up a lot of coffee shops, but they don't settle for an espresso in the movies. Often it leads them high into the mountains to find the Ancient One, the Sage, or the Guru who could redefine their life's struggle with a magic proverb.

I'm thankful for all the ones who have laid down a trail for me to follow. The steps I take everyday aren't ones I came up with. I am trying to follow in some big footsteps, but not because I'm after the one-off moment that will redefine everything. I want the everyday stuff that shows the kind of life Jesus hopes for all of us.

That's what my friend Greg found in the mountains. He didn't go in search of answers. He went because it was where love compelled him to go. He wasn't desperate to discover some secret that would change everything. He kept climbing the mountain one step at a time because he carried a truth that changed everything. Everyday with Jesus is better than any day without him.

When he reached the top of the mountain at Lampacoy Greg found a couple who already knew what it meant to put one foot in front of the other as they walked with Jesus. They did it everyday as they went about their lives. Jesus was with them as they harvested crops in a landscape that would make the farmers I know shrug in bewilderment. Jesus was with them as they experienced the heartache and tragedy all too common in such remote places.

There were no saints or sages on the mountaintop. There were no magic answers, just faithful reminders of the perfect answer. Everyday with Jesus is better than any day without him.

Greg learned to walk the same path with a new rhythm. Because he had learned it well, it became a place he liked to take his friends. Friends want one another to share the paths that become so special to them. I'm grateful for it. Everyday with Jesus is the best path we can share.

I've been on so many trails I couldn't even begin to remember them all, but I'll never forget the one Greg pointed out to me in Lampacoy. It's a rugged trail of hard packed dirt. It's not cut into the mountain. There are no steps to make the journey less treacherous. There are no handrails. It just goes straight up the side of the steep ascent.

It's not even a long hike. You can walk the whole thing in about twenty minutes. If you're in tip top shape you might not even have to throw up along the way.

On both sides of the trail are fields the mountain farmers spend their entire life planting and harvesting. The small tough men of those villages could teach us a lot about grit and determination in pursuit of goals. It is remarkable what they subject themselves to everyday in order to provide for their families.

Where the trail ended at the top of the mountain was a smooth dirt pad. It looked like the kind of place you might land a helicopter, but this was no helipad. In the middle of the pad stood a tall beautiful brown horse.

When I would come to his hilltop again on later trips he'd still be right there in the same place. I'm sure he made a trip or two; but it looked like he mostly just hung out on the same hill all the time never really wondering what was on the other side of the misty mountain vales perforating the landscape as far as the eye could see. It was beautiful in a breathtaking kind of way unrelated to the strenuous hike.

Every time I've been back I just stand there in wonder. That pinnacle on the mountain, next to the horse, on the crest that rose above the saintly Widow of Lampacoy is a sight that brings forth gratitude from the depths of my soul. I stand, and look, and think about all that Jesus did for me. I'm reminded of how good grace is. How could anyone doubt the goodness of God amidst a scene of such natural splendor?

Standing there I didn't just see the mountains, or the azure cloud kissed sky. Instead, I witnessed the vastness of a place it would take me decades to experience up close. So I whispered a prayer of thanks to God for a moment, on a hill, that captured the experience and reminded me of the importance of every step it took to get there.

IMPORTANT STEPS

I don't think Jesus would have had any problems walking up the trail in Lampacoy. He was pretty big on cardio. Have you ever noticed how much walking he seemed to do?

I don't know if any of his friends, the disciples, were out of shape guys—but I bet none of them knew what they were signing up for when he told them to follow him.

Jesus walked everywhere. He walked on roads. He walked from town to town. He walked in the wilderness. He walked to boats so they could take somewhere where he would walk some more. He walked up mountains. He even walked on water. His followers went with him. Everywhere Jesus went there were his friends.

It's a remarkable picture of the importance of every step. Jesus had asked them to follow him, and they did. But there was one walk they couldn't take with him.

The day Jesus was murdered on the cross was a pretty horrific day. But it was also a beautiful, wonderful turning point in history. The fate of humanity shifted with every step Jesus took that day.

At a kangaroo court the religious snobs rolled out their dog and pony show. Then Jesus was beaten within an inch of his life. He was stripped of his clothes, his flesh, and his dignity as the Roman torturer flayed him again and again.

Naked, bloodied, and beaten beyond human recognition the praetorians took it one step further. They unknowingly set up the Son of God for the steps that would change it all for everyone looking to spend everyday with Jesus. They laid an old marred timber on his ravaged back.

Jesus began to climb the hill. His every step leaking his life's blood from the many wounds. He kept going. It's hard to know what was on his mind at that moment, but I can't help thinking it was people like you and I.

Finally, his physical strength failed for the first time. He fell to the ground, spilling his cross onto the blood-soaked trail. To have come so far was remarkable. But he had further still to go. The Romans made a guy named Simon grab the cross and follow Jesus. Even on the walk to his death Jesus was helping people find ways to follow him.

It's hard to know for sure, but I doubt Simon woke up that day expecting to participate in the fate of the world. Did he know who Jesus was? It seems likely. Did he follow Jesus like Peter and the gang? Probably not.

What is made clear for us in the story of Jesus' crucifixion is that he did follow Jesus. He didn't *just* follow either. He participated. He picked up the cross and followed in the bloodied footsteps of the Son of God.

We don't know how far Simon walked with Jesus. We only know that he did. Even for a guy who hadn't been beaten nearly to death, carrying the cross could not have been easy. Did he slip in the bloodied mud of the trail? Was each trip a treacherous strain? Did the Romans give him a breather every so often? I doubt it.

For a moment in history Simon participated in the anguish of Jesus. His steps led him to the place where Jesus died. Further, Simon carried the implement of death itself. What does a memory like that do to a man? I'll have to ask him some day on the other side of eternity, but I wonder if from that day forward he remembered every bloody step?

LEAN IN

Jesus' friends who captured the story of that moment with the cross don't say anything about Simon trying to get away. He probably wasn't excited about being forced to participate in the death of the guy who healed people. But Simon didn't try to run away. Simon leaned in.

Have you ever had to carry something uphill? It's not an easy thing to do. Leaning in is the best way to go about it. You create leverage between your burden and your boots as you make your way forward. Simon leaned in.

It's impossible to know how Simon felt about what happened, but I'd bet he never forgot about it. I wonder if every hill he came to made him remember the hill he walked with Jesus. I wonder if he thought about the cross each time he picked up wood for his cookfire. Simon walked one afternoon with Jesus, but I'd bet it changed all of the afternoons that came later. Simon leaned in.

Every time I've stood on that far away hill starring out across the valley of Lampacoy it's given me a moment to think about the steps that got me there. Not just the steps up the side of the steep terrain; but the ones that put me on the airplane; the steps that took me toward a life of walking with Jesus. There gazing out over a place full of rugged beauty I'm touched by the beauty of the old rugged cross. The one Simon carried up a hill far away. The one where he learned how much a day with Jesus can change everything.

We have to answer the same question Simon must have pondered. What are you and I to do with that? How do we respond to the gratefulness one must sense for someone willing to give his life for you? What should we do when we begin to believe that everyday with Jesus is better than any day without him?

CHAPTER 9
ON A HILL

GATHER AROUND

I spent several minutes marveling at the stunning sight of the valley on my first hike up the mountainside. Eventually, I opened the black silver case I had carried to the top. Inside was a tiny helicopter that looked like a toy. But I didn't take it up the mountain to play. My drone came equipped with a camera.

I had already taken more pictures than I would ever look at, but for some reason felt compelled to fly my drone off the side of the mountain. I guess I thought the camera would capture what my eyes couldn't. It didn't. It's possible that I'm just a crummy drone pilot. I have buddies that capture amazing things with their drones; but all of my drone footage stunk. No single shot could capture what happened when my eyes looked on the real thing.

I didn't get any cool pics from my little drone, but

something else happened when I started buzzing it around all over the side of the mountain. Kids showed up. Dozens of them. It was almost like they had been hiding in the bushes. Maybe they were watching to see if the skinny white guy would puke from the hike up the mountain. I just turned around one moment and they were there, bunched together on the other side of the dirt pad.

I said, "Hi" and "hola" and smiled my big smile, but my Spanish was poor, and their English was nonexistent. So I did the only thing I could think of. I took my little drone and began to hover it in the air just a few feet off the ground in front of them. Their eyes grew wide and their mouths gasped in collective wonder. It was obvious none of them had ever seen anything like it before.

I moved it subtly up and down, back and forth, and side to side. They were transfixed. So then I zipped it away from them with all the speed the little electric motors could muster, hurtling over the edge of the hill to fly away. Disappointment darkened their little faces, but only momentarily because I already had it racing back to us. Then it was there between us again. They erupted in a smattering of cheers and excitement. I cut the engines and it fell a few inches before landing on my outstretched palm.

I held the small drone out toward the crowd of kids. They stood transfixed and unmoving. Until one of them understood. I guess he must have been about six years old. He took his first hesitant steps across the hilltop.

He left the crowd behind and moved toward my outstretched palm where the drone sat.

His buddies all looked on to see what would happen. I held my other hand up, first pointing at him, and then unfurling it with an empty palm up. He got the point as he lifted his small hand up and opened his waiting palm. I flicked the drone high into the air, dozens of little Guatemalan eyes lifting to see what would happen with baited breath. Before it could crash to the ground I snatched the controls and sent the small rotors into motion with a quick gesture I had practiced with my kids many times before. The kids all stood motionless, especially my new friend, his arm raised and hand outstretched—and then I landed the drone in his waiting palm. You would have thought he had just won the Super Bowl. The hill erupted in a cacophony of celebration.

What started in my palm made its way to his palm. To them it looked like magic. But to me it was just what drones do. They move from one place to another. They land where a hand is waiting.

That simple gesture became an unspoken invitation. For the rest of the day the kids followed me around. I totally abandoned my pursuit of filming with my drone. Instead I just flew it around playing with the kids.

Occasionally I would crash the drone into a tree and they'd all scurry into the bush to find it. The victor would emerge a momentary hero in the eyes of his friends.

Once I somehow managed to get the drone stuck on a piece of sheet metal when I landed it on a roof. Unfortunately it was the tallest roof in the village, and the structure was built on the side of the steep hill. So any effort to reach it was pointless. I wrestled at the controls for far too long before finally managing to wriggle it away from whatever held it down.

We played like this for what seemed like a long time. I would fly the drone. The bold kids would chase it. The shy kids would stand about ten feet away from me and watch. We were having a great time. I was completely absorbed in the moment with my new friends—all of us enjoying ourselves.

I had taken a case of extra batteries with me. Not the kind of batteries you pop in your flashlight. These were special batteries. They were unique to my drone. Each one was only good for fifteen minutes of sustained flight. So after a couple of hours I was running out of power.

I had been so absorbed in my fun with the kids that I hadn't noticed what was happening around me. After popping my last battery into the little slot on the bottom of the drone I looked up. It wasn't just kids watching anymore. People were everywhere, all over the hill. To my eyes it seemed like all the people had come to see what was happening on the hill.

Some had probably come to check on their kids. I bet some wanted to see what the stranger was up to. And probably more were interested in what was making all the commotion in their quiet mountain sanctuary. But, at some point they had all shown up. They didn't take their kids and leave. They gathered around to see what would happen.

Eventually I squeezed the last drop from the last battery. It happened mid-flight. The drone plunged thirty feet into the steepest cornfield I'd ever seen. People of all ages scrambled into the hillside rows to find the little gadget. A couple of minutes later a young man came sauntering up with a grin that covered his entire face. He held out the drone to me. Unbeknownst to him, the drone was broken.

LEADING THE CHARGE

The place where Jesus died on the cross is often called Calvary. As a kid the only reference I had for that were soldiers who rode horses into battle. It never really occurred to me to ask people why we called it Calvary. I kind of assumed it must have had something to do with a confusing part of the Bible where Jesus was riding a white horse.

Later I learned the truth. Calvary wasn't a place. Yeah, we had taken to calling a place Calvary. But it was kind of like calling where you go to watch a movie, "the movies". Movies aren't a place, they are an experience. A movie is not somewhere you go. It is something you experience.

Calvary is not somewhere Jesus went. It was something he experienced. Only because of his experience there was it first called Calvary. But what did Jesus experience there? High on the hill the locals called "The Place of the Skull" Jesus was murdered.

Simon had carried his cross until they reached the end of the line, Calvary. Jesus was lashed to two old used timbers. Ones no doubt used an untold number of times before to carry out the execution of criminals.

If you know the story you've no doubt heard people talk about the nails Jesus took for us. But they weren't your local hardware store kind of nails. Once they had his hands and feet tied down they took spikes and began to pound them into his flesh. These weren't the kind of nails your dad used to build your treehouse when you were a kid. They were brutal Roman spikes driven through the soft nerve centers and tissue of some of the most sensitive parts of the human body.

They tied him down to make the spikes do what they wanted. They nailed him to that tree to make the murder more efficient. They raised Jesus in the air to cause him to struggle for every breath.

His ravaged body would have struggled for every gasp. Each heartbeat would have been agonizing. The cross was so cruel and terrible a new word was invented to describe it—excruciating—meaning, out of the cross.

As Jesus suffered on the hill people gathered around. It was nothing like my joyful gathering on a mountain top hundreds of years later. No one laughed in joy, although some cruel people did laugh in apparent victory.

They mocked Jesus. They hurled insults. They spoke

of the many times he had saved others and dared him to save himself. Their arrogance demanded a final proof from the Son of God.

Jesus could have. He said as much. An army of heaven's angels crowded the hilltop circling the scene in the unseen realm. He could have called them to his aid. He could have rescued himself without their help. Instead, Jesus did what he's always done. He led the charge.

It wasn't the ropes they used to tie him down that held him there. It wasn't the metallic spikes driven through his joints that fixed him to the cross. It wasn't his failing body that kept him from coming down. It was you. It was me. It was everyone he knew would come to follow him.

Jesus allowed himself to be tortured. Jesus experienced excruciating physical, emotional, and even spiritual torment for us. He willingly endured. Calvary is where he led the charge.

Jesus was set up by the religious people who were jealous. He was murdered by the government out of indifferent misunderstanding. He was jeered by the crowd he had walked among. He hung there ravaged, decimated, and apparently defeated until his human heart could no longer endure the trauma it had suffered. It broke.

Jesus died of a broken heart, for us. That's what Calvary was, the place where Jesus gave his last natural human heartbeat away for you. His final moments were beyond anything we can imagine.

Jesus looked up. He said, " it is finished" and breathed his last breath. As he did his heart broke for you. It looked like the end. But it wasn't the end. All of Jesus' enemies cheered; but heaven started the countdown.

Jesus wasn't finished. He wasn't dead. He was leading the charge. Because only the Son of God could take on death itself.

DID WE WIN

His friends wrote down the stories about what happened that day because it was so surreal. It blew their minds. Not at first. At first they were terrified and confused. So they hid. Only later did they understand. Only after Jesus returned.

What Jesus did on the hill gathered a crowd. Just like he always did. At the end of the day what everyone had gathered to see was broken, but he wasn't finished.

Sometimes I hear well meaning people chastise the way Jesus' friends responded to his murder. They'll act as if they would have stuck it out like the disciple John. According to history he's the only guy who watched Jesus die. The rest of Jesus' buddies had scattered like troublemakers when the principal shows up.

Maybe some people would have had the temerity to stand on the hill surrounded by a mixed crowd of hostile antagonists, torturous soldiers, and mournful spectators. I'd love to say I would be like John. I'm pretty sure I would have been more like Thomas.

Thomas is the guy who catches a lot of grief when we tell this story. In fact people even started calling him Doubting Thomas. I think we should give Thomas some grace. The dude had a pretty rough week.

His friends had all scattered. His teacher had been murdered because the religious leaders and the government decided to form a surprise tag team. And now some ladies, and even Peter, had showed up to tell him Jesus wasn't really dead.

Put yourself in Thomas' position for a minute. My heart tells me I hope I could have been like John who stood at the foot of the cross and had a conversation with Jesus as he was dying. I would even take being like Peter who sprinted to the empty tomb that first Easter morning. But I have to admit I think I would have been more like Thomas.

I think I would have wanted to stay in a room surrounded by my friends. I think doubt may have gotten the best of me. Do you know why I think I'm like Thomas? Because there have been plenty of days when I find myself on Team Thomas.

I grew up hearing the story of Jesus told on a nearly daily basis. I grew up accepting it as reality. I believed it before I could really understand it. And then one day something unexpected happened. I came to understand what was supposed to have happened that long ago day on the hill far away at the place called Calvary.

It was only once I understood that doubt had a foothold. I found myself sitting at the table with Thomas instead of sprinting to the tomb with Peter. I found myself wondering how a man who died could reclaim his life of his own accord rather than standing at the foot of the cross like John. I doubted.

That's when Jesus showed up. I don't mean he walked through my bedroom wall and showed me his scars. Not the way he did with Thomas. He showed up in other ways, more meaningful ways for me.

I saw Jesus at work in the way my elderly uncle cared for his crippled wife. I watched Jesus change the heart of people I had prayed for for decades. I had a front row seat as Jesus changed the character of loved ones who had finally decided to live in his company.

As the people in my life changed, it reinforced my own trust in Jesus. I saw them living out what had become so important in my life—everyday with Jesus is better than any day without him. The reminder was a lifeline.

CHAPTER 10
UNDER YOUR MASK

OUR MASK

Jamie was in the store one day buying groceries for our family of six. As she meandered down the aisles she came across four people she knew greeting each one in turn. They all ignored her. Not a single one recognized her. Why? Because she was wearing a mask.

During the global Covid-19 pandemic it seemed like everyone was wearing masks. We wore masks because of health concerns. Or we wore them out of respect for those who asked us to. But some people live their lives under a mask.

We have all learned what it's like to wear masks. We all know what it's like to feel the pull of a mask. We all know what it's like to put on an appearance.

Sometimes we wear confidence, pretending like we are certain when we're not. We wear happiness acting like we are enjoying life when we are miserable or hurting. We wear perfection portraying a facade that nothing is wrong. We wear peace pretending to live in unity with those around us. We wear prosperity living like we are secure in material things.

When I was a kid this used to be called "putting on airs". Why? Because it's an empty and loveless way to live.

Living under your mask is an empty way to live. It's all surface level and no heart. It's hard to know someone if they are not authentic. An empty life is a loveless life. Do you want to live a life empty of love? No, of course not.

Jesus wants you to live from the center not the surface. We see the results of superficial living all around us. People are tired, divisive, lonely and so much more. Maybe you're experiencing some of that yourself. Perhaps you're starting to feel the effects of living under a mask. Or you've been feeling them for a while now.

When pain, shame, or trouble hits we are often tempted to go into lock down. We are uncomfortable dealing with discomfort. So we hide under our masks.

Living under a mask strips away our relationships. We are left with only the deep ones, people who really know us. Who knows you? That's hard to answer if you've been living under a mask.

HIDDEN LIFE

A hidden life is a tragic life. There are so many things people keep hidden. They keep it a secret.

In our house we like to say, "we don't do secrets—we do surprises". Why? Surprises are great! Secrets are poison.

You need people to know who is under your mask. Everything else is superficial. Superficiality is how we disguise our secrets. The life you live in secret is the mask you wear in public.

Jesus doesn't want that for you. He wants you to be known by others. He wants you to have a true life. A free life. He wants you to experience joy, peace, hope, confidence, faith, and love through connection to himself and other people.

Real love is *never* superficial. Love that only lives on the surface isn't actually love at all.

A long time ago a guy named Paul wrote about this in a letter to some friends in Rome. About twenty-five years earlier some Roman officials had crucified Jesus in a small province of the empire. It was a really big deal to everyone in the area; but in far away Rome no one had really noticed. To the few who had heard about it Jesus was just a criminal.

At the time Rome was a very superficial society. Paul's letter to the Roman Christians was different. It wasn't academic and it wasn't written in an office or library.

Paul's letter involved one big question. "What does

Jesus' resurrection mean for us?" He sorted out his answers on the road. Maybe while sailing or camping in the middle of nowhere. While he worked everyday at his trade just like you do.

Paul was wrestling with what it *really* meant to follow Jesus everyday. Why? Because Paul knew that everyday with Jesus is better than any day without him. His letter gives us a front row seat to his thoughts. It's pretty telling. Paul encouraged his friends to live without a mask. He said, *"Love from the center of who you are; don't fake it."* Paul understood this because he understood what Jesus wants for us. Jesus wants us to experience authentic human connection.

If someone close to you doesn't know your faults, your insecurities, your fears, and your desires you may only be living from the surface—not from the center. You might be faking it. Do you want to fake it? I don't think you do.

Experiencing the best part of what Jesus wants for you everyday involves your relationships. You have to have loving relationships. Relationships built on authenticity. You can't fake real love. Love from the center of who you are; don't fake it.

MINE

I was cooking one day and my daughter Anna wanted a bite of cheese. So I cut her a piece. She reached up and went "unn unnnn". I handed it over and she started to say something. I thought she was going to say *"Tane*

Too". That is *"Thank you"* if you don't speak Toddler. She reached for it and proclaimed, *"Mine!"* She wasn't bashful about it. She wanted me to know. Then she turned around and told her mom, *"Mine!"* She wanted Jamie to know. And then, she repeated it with each of her three brothers.

Jesus wants you to have people you can look at and declare some things to. He wants you to be close enough to them and close enough to him to be able to get honest about it. He wants you to say, "This is mine!" This is my hope for my family. This is my plan for my future. This is my pain I need help with. This is my promise to you.

But we will never have anyone we can share our life with if we don't love from the center of who we are. Love from the center not the surface.

Jamie and I bought some really funny masks right after we got married. They were for a Halloween party back when we spent most of our time with college students. One was an old man covered in wrinkles with a giant nose and huge gray beard that hung to my chest. The other mask was a grandmotherly mask with her short gray hair held up in a bun.

One day I walked up behind Jamie as I was telling her something. She didn't know I had my mask on. She was like "I can't understand you!" When she turned around in frustration and saw it she actually jumped.

If you live under a mask you will never be understood. You need to be known. You need to be understood. It's a big part of what Jesus wants for you everyday.

So let me challenge you with something. Talk to a friend or your spouse. Tell them how you're really doing and what you really want. Let them see under the mask. Let them know what is really making you tick. What you are hoping for. Tell them what you dread. Explain your fears and your dreams. Words passed between friends move love toward the center instead of the surface. That's a great start.

RUN

Jesus wants you to have real relationships. He wants to be part of your everyday life. But he uses other people to make that known to us. What else can we do to get out from under our mask? How do we do it? How do we love from the center and not the surface?

Paul's friends asked the same kinds of questions. His answer was this, "Run for dear life from evil; hold on for dear life to good. Be good friends who love deeply; practice playing second fiddle."

This is the *do* part. I don't know about you, but I am incredibly grateful that Paul shared how to do this. Spending your days living out what Jesus wants for us aren't as hard or complicated as you may have believed.

Run for dear life from evil. In other words, move toward good. If something is evil—move in a different direction. If something is good—move toward that.

The big stuff Jesus wants to do in your everyday life always begins when we move toward good and away from evil. Not because we are perfect, but because we are aiming at what Jesus wants for our everyday life. Not because we are better than anyone else; but because we want what's best for our everyday life. Not because we have everything figured out; but because we want to move toward the one who does. And—when enough people move toward good and away from evil that's a movement. A movement is a lot of people moving toward Jesus.

I used to hear this phrase a lot as a kid. "Flee from the very appearance of evil." Why? Because if you keep moving toward evil you'll be so close to it, even if you're not participating it will look like you are.

Have you ever known someone who loved flirting with crossing the line between good and evil? That is the appearance of evil. It's like saying, "I want to *be* good, but *look* bad." It sounds ridiculous. Living with Jesus everyday means moving *away* from that.

My life will reflect what I'm moving toward. It becomes my mask. Anger, selfishness, dissension, unforgiveness, and bitterness creeps in if we drop our guard. We need to be careful. We need to move away from evil.

HOLD ON

Several months ago we kept hearing a crazy noise downstairs at night. Jamie woke me up shouting, "did you hear that crash in the garage?" She was convinced someone was breaking into our car. I jumped out of bed and went to the garage; but there was nothing happening.

Two days later we came home to sawdust all over the carpet. It was weird. Why in the world would there be sawdust on our floor? And then we found the possum.

Yes, a possum was in my house. I have no idea how it got in there. We looked for hidden holes in the house for days. Nothing. Nevertheless, when I walked in that day there was a possum staring up at me with his little beady intruder eyes.

Do you know what I didn't do? I didn't say, "welcome to the King Casa little buddy." Do you know what I did? I walked up to him and said, "it's time for you to go." And then I picked it up by the tail and carried it outside.

Be careful what you let in. There's a lot of stuff trying to sneak into your home right now. Lately there's been a massive shift in abuse, addiction, suicide, violence, depression, anxiety and more. This list keeps going.

It's critically important you and I get this right. Not because we can be perfect, but we can stop embracing evil. We can move in a different direction. The one Jesus wants for us everyday. Instead of embracing evil we can "hold on for dear life to good."

We can hold on and not let go. If something is good in your life. Keep it around. Fight for it. Treasure it. Let it take the center stage. Jesus is the amazing first step for those of us trying to get this right. Authentic relationships are a huge part of it.

When the possum showed up I only held onto it long enough to get it out of my life. And then I moved away. Do you know what the possum didn't do? It didn't try to follow me back to the house. It understood it was unwelcome. Uninvite the things in your life that don't belong. Throw wide the gates for those that do. Start with Jesus. Add friends.

Be a good friend who loves deeply. Let people know you. You should know them. If you know someone but they don't know you, you're not a friend, you're a fan. A good friendship goes both ways.

If someone knows you, but you don't know them, stop dumping on them all of the time. Let them see under the mask. Love from the center not the surface.

Get a lot of practice playing second fiddle. Be good at not being the most important person in your own life. If the direction of your life's compass is always pointing at you—you stink at playing second fiddle. Stop hogging the spotlight. The spotlight always wants to shine on the superficial when it points at us. You'll know you're playing second fiddle when you're always trying to push someone else into the spotlight.

The more you try to push someone else toward the spotlight the more people you'll inevitably gather around you. Authenticity creates opportunities for the best that love has to offer. So, love from the center not the surface.

When you're not living under the crushing weight of superficial love you will no longer be the most important person in your own life. As you move away from evil the people who truly know you will be compelled to come along with you. Why? Because you've become someone who helps them move toward what Jesus wants for them, too.

Living in the company of friends who know each other and want what's best for one another is exactly what Jesus wants for all of his friends. He wants it for you, me, the guy that changes your tires, and everyone else you know.

Where do we begin? The same place my friend Roger did. By recognizing that we need help and reaching out to someone who knows us.

Jesus didn't die so he'd have fans. He came to build a kingdom full of friends. People who would take off their masks and really love one another. Brave souls willing to love everyday from the center of who they are and who Jesus is helping them become.

CHAPTER 11
RUN TOGETHER

MY FIRST RACE

The first time I ran a long distance race I was 33 years old. All of my life I had been an athlete. I was always the guy in shape in my friend group. I was the guy that could swim like a dolphin, the one who grew up working on a farm and could outlast everyone else. Until one day when I wound up in a full court basketball game in the Dominican Republic. That day was a real struggle.

I went home and said, "I'll never be that out of shape again." And I haven't been because I started running. I'd get up early every morning pushing my oldest son Ethan in a stroller. He would sleep while I would run.

At first I couldn't even run a mile. Eventually I did it. Soon I could do three, five, seven, ten, and then even fourteen miles. My cousin thought all that running was crazy. He said, "Boy, if you ever see me running you better run, too."

So I ran. I got in shape. I was nailing it. I was doing well. Making all kinds of progress.

The training continued for a year. Then I signed up for a race.

When race day came I felt great. I had a team of friends from church running with me. I was excited. It was going to be so fun.

When the horn sounded we all took off. The super humans took off at super human speed. The regular humans took off at regular human speed. And the slow humans took off at my speed. I remembered my training. I wasn't on a basketball court anymore. There wasn't any good reason to sprint. This wasn't the soccer pitch, no one was waiting to loft a high floating kick for a header into the goal. I had to pace myself. Even with all of my training the urge to compete hammered at my resolve. I didn't want to run. I wanted to win.

As we progressed through the checkpoints people handed us cups of water and orange slices. *How nice.* I thought. *I wish someone would hand me breakfast when I was out here training.* As the race progressed the competition seemed to thin. We weren't clumped up anymore like we had been in the beginning. We were spread out. A few of the superhumans rocketed toward the finish, leaving all of us regular humans in their wake.

Going into the last mile I was really feeling it. I was tired. Every footfall felt like I was dragging sneaker-clad weights, but I refused to be left behind. I didn't realize just how tired I was until I looked up and this old guy was leaving me in the dust. I was steadily putting one foot in front of the other. At this point in the race I was scraping the bottom of the barrel, laying out everything I had. And then here came the old guy, passing me like I had stopped to tie my shoes. The worst part is, he was walking. *He was walking!* There went all of my aspirations as a runner.

It took me thirty three years and getting passed by a geriatric walker to learn something I'm pretty sure Jesus had been trying to get through my thick head for years. You have to run your own race.

THE CLOUD

Have you ever been tired? I don't mean the kind of tiredness you get after a big lunch. Nor am I talking about the tiredness you might feel after missing a decent night of sleep. Have you ever been really tired?

When we go beyond being merely tired to be truly tired a shift happens inside. The daily stuff becomes challenging beyond what we can imagine. When that happens we don't want a nap, or even a break, we often want to just unplug from the world and hide until it goes away. Unfortunately, hiding won't make it go away.

Decades after the first small group took off in Peter's house a letter was written to another group of believers. Scholars aren't entirely sure who wrote the letter. But they are pretty sure it was written to a group of Hebrew people who had experienced years of persecution, execution, torture, and disdain. People who were tired.

The Hebrew letter is full of stuff we could learn about living everyday with Jesus. Near the end is a chunk that reminds me of the day I ran my first race. It talks about being surrounded by a large group of people watching you. There's a good reminder that to win the race we have to set aside the stuff that drags us down or trips us up. Most of all, we have to run the race in front of us with endurance.

Some of you reading this are tired. You are tired of hearing people squabble all the time. You are tired of life just seeming to be a constant series of hardship. Perhaps, you're tired of the way it makes you overreact to things. Maybe you're tired of a society that seems hell bent on rejecting the Jesus you desperately want to walk with daily. Or, you are simply tired of wondering what kind of world your kids will grow up in. If you're tired you're in good company. We all get tired.

When the Hebrew writer was writing to his tired friends what did he remind them? He reminded them they weren't meant to run alone. Life with God isn't a solo endeavor.

Hey, guess what? You weren't meant to run alone. Everyday with Jesus is better than any day without him. Do you know what sweetens the deal? The ones who run with you.

You need a family of faith cheering you on. The guy who wrote the letter called it a "cloud of witnesses". That sounds like a bunch of friends who showed up to cheer you on. The cloud of witnesses encourages you. The cloud of witnesses props you up. They pray with you and for you. The cloud of witnesses has your back. Your cloud of witness corrects you. They surround you. We all need God's people gathered around us. We all need to be around God's people.

You can run the race by yourself, but you'll run your best race in the company of friends. With God's people is how you run the best race. With your cloud of witnesses.

LIFE GIVING

I don't run for exercise anymore, but I'm still moving. I didn't get out of shape. I just got older. I switched it up. One day my doctor looked at me and said, "Never run again."

I told him, "You're underpaid."

I had stopped running before my doctor told me I needed to, but I took my doctor's words to heart. Do you know why? Because I know him. He's not just a guy in a white coat. He's a man I trust.

As my doctor he is poised to literally be "life-giving". It's in his job description. As a guy who spends everyday with Jesus his voice is one I trust to speak into my life.

You should have some voices you trust. Who's in your cloud? Those are the healthy relationships you trust to speak into your race. When you're tired, dragging, or struggling the cloud compels you to keep on running. Far too many people seem to confuse the cloud for some other kind of relationship.

There are only three kinds of relationships: giving relationships, taking relationships, and healthy relationships. Avoid the first two and aim your heart at the third one.

In a giving relationship all you do is give to the other person. Those are so dangerous. Get out of them. They will kill your joy, and ruin your life. If you're in one, run!

In taking relationships all you do is take from the other person. Those are selfish. Don't be selfish. People spending everyday with Jesus aren't supposed to be selfish. If you're a taker the other person needs to run from you.

In either case, If it's all give or all take—get away, yesterday. That's not a relationship. It is abuse.

Thankfully, there are also healthy relationships. In a healthy relationship there is some give and some take. You give what the other person needs and you take what you need. Together you make each other better. The best relationships work this way. They are life-giving.

A life-giving relationship is a connection with someone spending everyday with Jesus. Look for others who know everyday with Jesus is better than any day without him. When you find them you've found your "cloud of witnesses".

Relationships are good for you, but this is so much more than that. Broccoli is good for you, but you can get calcium, iron, and Vitamin C somewhere else—all the broccoli haters said, "Amen". Running is good for you, but you can exercise a million ways. If you want to learn a few of them follow my friend Brett on instagram. Even reading your Bible is critical for you, but you could listen to it. You can only get life-giving relationships from one source, people.

You need it. I need it. They need it. People need people.

Life-giving relationships spur us on. Have you ever ridden a horse? It has been a really long time since I was on a horse. The last time I rode a horse no one gave me spurs. Probably because I wasn't good enough at riding to control an animal running at top speed.

A life-giving friend is able to spur you enough to get you moving! It's not mean. It is healthy. We don't spur one another on toward hate and bad decisions! We urge each other toward love and good deeds. With a friend's encouragement you can handle life at the speed of friendship.

HOW DOES IT WORK

Our church does this through groups. It's one of the main ways we learn how to spend everyday with Jesus. We hold close to a deep belief that you need friends you know well, but who also know you well.

During the Covid19 pandemic we wanted to be careful about passing potential sickness around from house to house. So we took a break for a little while. I'll never forget the day we brought them back. It was such an amazing day! It was like the most important part of our church was back.

Spend everyday with Jesus. Everyday with him really and truly is better than any day without him. If you're doing it right, more than a few of those days will be Sundays. When Sunday rolls around I hope you find yourself in a cloud of witnesses. I hope you gather around friends and Jesus in a way that equips you to live daily for Jesus. But Sundays are not enough.

You need everyday with Jesus. Do you know what happens to people if they only eat once a week? They starve to death. They slowly die.

Finding your cloud of witnesses is about making you stronger. It's where you can work out what God is doing in your life. It's the friends you can call on when you need someone. Please, don't pass up the chance to find life-giving friends.

For the Church to be healthy we have to be more than people who sit in a room together and sing. The Church has to be more than a collection of people listening to encouraging stories. We have to be a place where people find their friends. The Church is supposed to be a launch pad for the cloud of witnesses.

It can be really challenging at first. So many people have been hurt by churches. The truth is people are mean. Some are deeply disingenuous. Don't let stand-outs cause you to miss out. That's like skipping a wedding because of the bride's sketchy uncle. Don't give up. Run together. Persist.

ASSUMPTIONS

We've all heard the dangerous potential of assumptions and what they can do to us. *Don't make assumptions*, conventional wisdom says. I say, toss that out. Make all kinds of assumptions. Make the right assumptions. People who don't like making assumptions just haven't found someone to make the right assumptions about.

One of the great things about finding your cloud of witnesses is that they will assume the best about you. You can assume the best about them.

The truth is, we're all jacked up. If you're sitting with three people the one on your left is jacked up. So is the one on your right. The one in the middle is just like them.

Because we are all flawed, we don't walk around with our noses up. It's impossible to follow Jesus if you're busy patting yourself on the back. I know how screwed up I am. When I forget my wife is there to remind me. We need to acknowledge our flaws without dwelling on them. Instead, we bring them to Jesus. Do it in the company of friends.

Your cloud of witnesses is where you can talk about it. It's where you can get help and advice. Sometimes my kids tick me off and I say something hurtful. I can go to my friends and ask other parents how they handled it. Sometimes I just can't bring myself to make the right choice. I can go to my cloud of witnesses and share the experience with others who do it, too.

Something truly remarkable begins to happen when

you share your problems with friends. When you're tired and facing your struggles in good company you build character.

Who do you want to finish with? Who are you going to finish with? I hope you don't finish your race any time soon. But I hope you find the ones you want to finish it with.

When the old guy passed me in the final mile of my first race it could have been really discouraging. I was demoralized, tired, and humiliated. Just as my disappointment got all tangled up with my expectations and fatigue Matt showed up. One second I was alone getting lapped by a geriatric walker, the next step I was running in the company of a friend. We finished the race together. We finished the race strong.

Guess what? Matt beat me. He had a faster time than I did. But somehow the timekeepers messed up and gave me first place in my age division. Matt was so cool about it. He didn't correct them. He just celebrated his friend.

When you find your cloud of witnesses you will find friends who celebrate you. The ones who will assume the best about you. Find some friends who are living everyday with Jesus.

CHAPTER 12
HEROES AND VILLAINS

ALL BARK

Every once in a while a guy with a bullhorn would show up at the university where I taught. He'd just randomly show up and yell at people for hours. He always wore a sandwich sign, and just stood there telling everyone exactly how they were going to go to hell. Having this guy around was like oral surgery for your ears.

When leaders in our community would go to speak with him, he would condemn them to hell. If a well meaning student would try to speak the truth, the guy with the signs would insist they were going to hell. He would point at people in the crowd and begin accusing them of all kinds of things one at a time.

According to this guy, cheerleaders were going to hell, the softball team was going to hell, the landscaping team mowing the grass was going to hell, everybody was destined for hell. I never once heard him talk about anyone who was getting it right. I never once heard him talk about Jesus. I certainly never heard him point anyone toward the loving truth and grace of Jesus.

Listening to the guy with the sandwich sign and the bullhorn yell accusations at everyone wasn't helpful for anyone. If that's all you ever heard about God you would never know Jesus loved you. You certainly wouldn't know Jesus wanted you to live your life with him daily. There was nothing in the guy's message to suggest that everyday with Jesus is better than any day without him. There was no grace, there was no truth, there was only a lot of angry yelling.

One of the nicknames given to the devil in the Bible is "accuser". It's not like a prison name someone gave him because God locked him up. It's almost more like a functional title.

When you go to the doctor you are first helped by a nurse. They are there to nurse you back to health. If you need help doing taxes you hire an accountant because they know how to account for every dollar. But no one asked for an accuser.

God didn't establish the enemy of your soul. He didn't set him up to be your accuser. Nevertheless, he is there, daily, accusing you. Take heart, just like the annoying guy with the bullhorn, accusation is all he's got on you.

My dog loves to bark anytime someone comes into our yard. She will go nuts with the barking, but I'm convinced she would never bite someone. How do I know? I tested it on an annoying neighbor. I know that doesn't sound like it lines up with the whole "love your neighbor as yourself thing," but actually it does. Because my dog had never bitten me I was pretty sure she wouldn't bite my neighbor. So, one day when she started barking I turned her loose to see what she would do.

She ran right up to the neighbor, barking. Then she stopped about ten feet away, tucked her nub of a tail down, and just crouched on the ground. Suddenly all the accusations were gone. She was all bark.

The devil is real. He is tossing a lot of accusations your way. Sometimes he whispers them in your ear. He lobs them toward heaven bitterly wishing for something to stick, but guess what? He's all bark. All bark? Wouldn't the devil be more of a cat guy? Probably, but all meow sounds a lot easier to ignore.

Is he occasionally right about something? Sure. We are not perfect. We are certainly flawed. But the devil isn't the bad guy in our story. People give the devil way too much credit.

Whatever character hangups are going on in your life aren't there because he orchestrated it like some dastardly supervillain plot. It happened because you did it. When we begin to understand our sin is our fault is when we can begin to grasp our ability to change.

CHANGE

Everyday I get questions from people all over the world. They run the gamut for both uniqueness and sincerity. But one kind of question shows up everyday, "Nate, how do I change?"

Some want to know how to change their thoughts. Many want to know how to drop a bad habit. Sometimes people just want me to play referee in their lives and tell them what they are doing is good or bad. They want an outside perspective to help them decide if they should change something about themselves.

I've spent my entire life around well-meaning folks trying their best to live with Jesus. All of the important people in my life growing up were those who lived it out sincerely. They truly understood that everyday with Jesus is better than any day without him.

I've also spent a lot of time around people who don't get Jesus. They only know about Baby Christmas Jesus. Or maybe a movie their grandma made them watch one time about Jesus getting beat up and killed.

There is a repeating statement I've heard again and again from both people following Jesus and the ones who don't even know what that means. I'm willing to bet you've heard this statement, "the devil made me do it." It's what people say when they want to blame some cosmic scapegoat. It's like a tongue in cheek way to say, "Oops, I know I shouldn't have done that, but it's not really my fault. I'm innocent."

I believe there is a devil. Why? Because my favorite

book, the Bible, makes it pretty clear the devil exists. I believe the devil is out there somewhere plotting against us. I believe the devil hates us because of how much God loves us. I also think the devil is not nearly as capable as many want to believe.

You know what? We give him way too much credit. I refuse to give the devil credit for the stupid things I do. He's all bark. He's not that strong. He's not that powerful. And, yes, sometimes this educated hillbilly is really dumb.

One of the first steps toward change is to stop passing the blame. Don't think of your failings and shortcomings as some kind of bad credit.

REAL HELL

This is an unpopular opinion in our day and age, but hell is real. And people who die without following Jesus wind up there. Guess what? The devil didn't make them do it.

It wasn't some red suited villain with a pointed tail and pitchfork holding you at gunpoint that made you drive across town to meet your girlfriend while your wife sat at home with the kids. And if it was, why didn't you call the cops?

We're way too prone to blame the boogie man or the bad guy. Everybody wants a villain in their story. Because a villain is their scapegoat. We think if we have a villain to blame we won't be held accountable for what we do.

Here is a reality check. We are accountable for what we do. It's our fault. Your bad habits are not the culmination of hell's machinations against you. Stop giving the devil credit.

Do I believe he can influence? Sure. But he isn't the one making your decisions for you. You chose to cheat on your taxes. You chose to explode in anger. You chose to step out on your wife. You chose to hide in a room in your house and give in to your porn habit.

Here is the really uncomfortable truth too many of us don't want to admit. In our story we are the bad guy. We're the villain. *That's harsh, Nate.* And, it is also true.

The devil isn't the one making you and I do the things we do. He is the bratty kid standing in the corner waiting to run off and tell the teacher. And, he is also the punk who spends the rest of your life reminding you about it.

While I realize that will be a hard pill for many to swallow, I'm hoping it will actually encourage many of us. How is *that* supposed to encourage me? You might be thinking. Once you know who the villain is all you have to do is set them up to face the hero. Because the hero *always* wins.

Newsflash! Jesus is the hero.

If you want to beat the villain in the mirror, go face to face with Jesus. Embracing what Jesus wants *for* you is the way to counteract what so many want to blame the devil for.

You *can* decide to put down your bad habits. You *can* decide to make changes to your life. You *can* decide to cut the unhelpful influences out of your life. You *can* decide to stop blaming someone else. You *can* decide to stop giving your accuser a timeslot on your calendar. You *can* decide to follow Jesus daily.

KEEPING SCORE

One of my mentors used to say, "there is a heaven to gain and a hell to shun." For a lot of people I have known the reality of that statement has left them in a nearly constant state of psychological stress. If you believe hell is real and people go there and you believe the same about heaven it can show up in your life like some kind of religious scorecard.

I've known a lot of people who live this way. They start doing things like counting their sins. They think maybe if I read my bible more than I sin I'll be okay. That's not how it works.

I've often wondered if we wind up thinking this way because of all the accusations we let into our lives. Don't let thoughts about the bad stuff play on repeat like an old record. Your walk with Jesus isn't about counting steps. It's not building up good credit versus bad credit. If you want to really follow Jesus everyday, cut that kind of thinking out of your life right now.

Hell is real. You have an accuser. And yes, you are the villain in your story.

But heaven is real, too. You have truth and grace on your side. They took shape that first Christmas morning as a baby in a manger. All of heaven's hope leveraged against the pitiful barking of the accuser and our own villainy.

There's not a magic cosmic scoreboard tracking your daily progress. Instead, there is someone who wants to help you take the next right step. The work of Jesus was heroic in every sense of the word.

Like that old guy said in one of the Batman movies, "he's the hero we need, not the one we deserve." But the hero we need isn't Batman. A guy running around in a suit pounding on people's heads sounds like the other guy.

Jesus is the hero we need. He's a better hero. Cheesy? Probably. True? Without a doubt.

It takes a real hero to walk into our lives and face the stuff we struggle to face ourselves. He has the strength to do it. He has the will and the desire to do it. He loves us so much he has been waiting for his chance to change everything. Because Jesus doesn't show up in our lives like a costumed super power—he goes where he's invited.

The twist in the story is that in order to defeat the villain in the mirror you need help from the outside. Jesus is that help, but you have to invite him to do it.

If it sounds weird, or overly simple, it isn't. It starts with a simple realization that you do truly need Jesus. What comes next is just as simple. You say, "Jesus, will you help me?"

The moment you make that decision all of heaven is leveraged in your favor. That is when you will begin to realize everyday with Jesus is better than any day without him. That is when your life will change.

Love is louder than anything the devil can say. The love God has for you. The grace Jesus brings your way. Your life was never meant to be about taking one more shot at the buzzer hoping you will get it right. So, stop keeping score. Tear down the scoreboard. It's not a thing of points or innings. It's a matter of course. The course Jesus wants for you is everyday with him. The beautiful thing about that is how he wants to help you make it happen.

CHAPTER 13
A BAD FRIEND

BAD FRIENDS

Recently I was reading a book about a guy who went to work one Monday morning. It was the same job he'd had for years. And while it wasn't his favorite job he did like the guys he did it with. They had become his closest friends.

One day during a routine stop they halted their van down the block from a bank as they were making their rounds. The driver looked up as his buddy tossed him a small bundle.

"What's this?" the driver said as it landed in his lap.

"Put it on and let's go," was all his friend said.

As the guy opened the bundle he saw it was a set of faded coveralls like guys wear who work on cars a lot. But that wasn't all. There was also a mask. With a sense of dread and bewilderment the driver hurriedly put the stuff on. Finally, as they stepped out of the van there was one last piece of the puzzle to play. His friend handed him a shotgun. They were there to rob the bank.

Do you have any bad friends? Most of us have had a bad friend at some point. They are the ones who get us into trouble.

I'm not talking about the normal childlike mischief we seem to all wander into as kids. I'm talking about real trouble. The "Let's smash all the mailboxes in our neighborhood!" kind of trouble. No, I've never done that. Probably because when I was growing up there was only one mailbox in the neighborhood. Mine!

Even so, I didn't escape the effect of bad friends. No one with bad friends escapes the touch they can leave on your life. Usually, the longer you hang around a bad friend the more ammo you're saving up for regret somewhere down the trail.

One of my childhood friends was a bad friend. He was always trying to get me to do stuff I knew I shouldn't do. This seemed to happen everytime we were together. And for a span of about six years we were together all of the time. Until finally one day our hobbies and interests took us in different directions. We were never really around each other much after that. Which is good because later he went to jail for being a robber.

I hope you have good friends around you. I am extremely fortunate to have made some wonderful friends in my life. Many of my friends—especially my closest friends all know that everyday with Jesus is better than any day without him.

The thing about friends is that they are powerful. They can affect your life in so many ways. I am enthusiastic about my belief that Jesus wants everyone following him to have great friends. I'm also convinced he wants us to avoid bad friends.

Bad friends will lead you to a bad life. Paul, another guy who knew everyday with Jesus is better than any day without him had quite a lot to say in some letters he wrote to his friends. Later these letters would find their way into our Bible because they are so important. In one of Paul's letters he said something pretty profound about friends. Paul said, "Bad company corrupts good character."

Way too many of us have found that to be true first hand. As is often the case, it's a hard way to learn an important truth. The people I know who have learned this truth would never sign up to live their life in the company of a bad friend. If you desire to be of good character you're not the kind of person looking for friends to rob banks with. Still, it's tragic how many people I know who love Jesus and pursue having good character, and yet they still spend way too much of their lives in the company of an equally bad friend called Regret.

Nate, do you have any regrets? I love this question because I can honestly say I have no regrets. It's not because I am perfect. So far from it. It's not because I'm naive concerning my mistakes, failures, and faults. It's because I don't give them permission to dictate my future.

I don't regret any of my bad relationships because they remind me how blessed I am now. I don't regret waiting so long to have kids because they are being raised by the best version of me. I don't regret my many many mistakes because the mess they made of my life became the message that helps so many. I don't regret becoming a pastor because the Good News is worth sharing. I don't regret becoming a teacher because learning changes lives.

Regret leaves us longing for what was. Jesus shows us how to be thankful for where we are. Regret leaves us full of empty wishes. Jesus shows us how to wish everyone could find grace in him. Regret has us longing to take back a few steps. Jesus fills us with hope for the next step.

DON'T BE EDITH

According to some ancient Jewish tradition there was a lady named Edith. Although her name isn't mentioned in the Bible there is a story about her. It's not a happy story. It's the story of a lady who's life comes to a terrifying and tragic end in the company of a bad friend. You guessed it. Regret did Edith in.

According to the story Edith was fleeing a terrible place with her family. The city was literally falling down around them, but God had hatched an escape plan for her and her loved ones. The plan came with a really important warning, "Don't look back."

They were doing okay. The plan seemed to be going

off without a hitch. When all of a sudden Edith did what way too many of us do. She looked back.

Like something straight out of a scary movie when Edith looked back she turned into a pillar of salt. She was frozen, forever, in the act of perpetual regret. All because she looked back. Regret really is the worst friend.

It's easy to read Edith's story and want to point fingers. It's easy to sit on the sidelines of history with the hindsight of hundreds of years of wisdom and learning and say things like, "why did she look back?", "that was dumb," "I wouldn't do that." There's a long list of statements you and I both hear from people when they think they are doing better at breaking up with Regret than Edith did. But not looking back on our own mistakes means not pointing fingers at someone else's either.

When Jesus did talk about the mistakes of his friends he didn't wield them like something to make them feel bad. He spoke about them in a way that was full of both grace and truth. Because Jesus is always full of truth he didn't make the bad stuff sound better than it really was. Jesus always talks about what's bad without trying to soften the reality through colorful language. But, also, because Jesus is so good he doesn't stop there.

Jesus would be a hard friend to live with if he just turned around and pointed out all of our mistakes with nothing but truth on his lips all of the time. Because Jesus is a great friend he does tell us the truth. But, because is such a great savior he does what no one else can do. He simultaneously covers each and every moment in grace.

The truth of what we have behind us would leave us ruined. It would leave us like Edith. Locked up, with nowhere to go, only fixated in our past.

The truth of what Jesus makes possible for us leaves us ready. Ready for the next step. We look up, with everywhere to go, fixated on what comes next.

With Regret every step becomes a painful exercise in distancing yourself from something you want to do all over again. Maybe you want to try to do it better. Maybe you want to go back and take another swing at a different option. All I know is Regret is a bad friend that leaves you living in the past.

When Edith looked back she thought about what she was giving up. Not what she was leaving behind. Trying to live in yesterday is a terrible way to live. It's also impossible. All it does is leave you stuck. Instead, don't look back.

LOOKING BACK

One night I was talking with a group of men. We were eating pizza and swapping stories when one of them brought up his regrets. The details could have been pulled from a cop show on TV. And just by the way he spoke about it I could tell he'd spent a long time hanging out with regret.

The effect regret had on my buddy is the same it

wants to have on anyone. Regret would have you spend all of your time looking back. People who live with regret are prone to statements like, "I wish I could do it all over again," "I wish I had never made that mistake," and "I wish I had never gone there that night." Regret loves to leave you wishing for things it can never give you.

Do you know what a wish is? A wish is a dream without action. Regret will never act on your behalf. Why? Because regret is a bad friend. Regret has no power to change anything about your past. Instead, regret is poised to always seize the next opportunity to have you waste your future. A lot of great people spin their wheels trying to chase down their regrets.

That's not how Jesus does it, which is exactly what I told my friend over pizza. We talked about how Jesus didn't wish for him to experience any of those things he had come to regret. I wanted him to know that even though those things had happened Jesus didn't write him off as wasted potential.

I shared an amazing statement found in the bible, "Jesus is the same, yesterday, today, and forever." This truth has given me courage, made me at peace, and showed up like a dump truck full of grace in the midst of my hard times. It's a statement one of Jesus' friends made that simply means this, "Jesus is always the same."

Simply put, Jesus is constant. I know this feels like stepping into the deep end of the pool for a second, but go with me. Jesus doesn't change. He isn't affected by the way time works in our lives because he is the same —always. In fact, one of the promises found in the bible that has always given me strength says that Jesus was always meant to die for us, even before the earth was formed. I know that can all seem a bit trippy and brainy. It seems hard to believe and lean into if it's not something you've ever really considered. Especially if you've never thought about what it means for you personally.

Here's where this hard to grasp truth becomes rock solid for me. Because I believe Jesus is the same always I believe Jesus never changes. Are you still following? Good! Because Jesus never changes he is the same Jesus right now, today, that he was on the day when I made my biggest mistake.

Jesus didn't turn a blind a eye to the thing you've been allowing Regret to throw in your face all of these years. And he wasn't surprised by it the day you finally decided to ask for his help. Jesus has been right there, everyday, waiting for the moment you would give your regrets to him. Everyday with Jesus really and truly is better than any day without him.

He is the same yesterday, today, and forever. So what we're looking back and longing for—he's always been hoping we'd get past. Jesus was there when the thing we would later look back on took root in our lives. And, in that moment he was already cheering for the day we'd see it as a testimony instead of a tragedy. He was looking ahead to the moment we could remember and rejoice rather than regret.

A BETTER FRIEND

I don't hang out with regret. Do you know why? Because regret is a BAD friend. Regret wants you to look back and see all your failures.

Jesus is a better friend. Jesus wants you to look back and see what he's done. What has Jesus done?

Jesus has turned the broken pieces of our lives into a mosaic of grace. He lifts each tarnished moment from our past, cleans it off, and gently places it into something amazing. Everyday with Jesus becomes another piece sliding together to tell the story of what he has done. What used to read as a highlight reel of bad decisions, character flaws, and willful rebellion is refashioned into an epic story of trust, grace, and following him. He truly turns our mess into a message worth sharing.

While Regret gets busy pointing fingers Jesus sheds his light on a truth he hopes for all mankind. Everyday with Jesus is better than any day without him. Even the days we feel like we've already bombed are better when remembered through the lens of grace. It's not at all like living through rose-colored glasses or naive indifference —it's deference.

We don't trust Regret because we know there's nothing good waiting for us in the company of such a bad friend. We do trust Jesus because we know there's nothing bad waiting for us in the company of the perfect friend. The difference is found in deference. Submit to Regret and you'll spend your life looking in the rearview mirror wishing to go in reverse. Submit to Jesus and you'll spend your life moving forward in the company of some grace-given wisdom.

We don't give Regret the microphone and put him on center stage. We save that spot for Jesus and the new story he wants for our lives. The everyday story Jesus will tell when he takes center stage. It's a better story from beginning to end.

CHAPTER 14
THE FOG

FRIDAY

My nephew died on a Friday. He was only twenty one years old. And every molecule of me hurt over it.

I hurt for my brother and sister in law who are such kind people. I hurt for my wife. I hurt for my oldest son who looked up to him. Death hurts. There's no sugar coating that. There's nothing cute that can be said.

It isn't as if his passing were a sudden thing, or even a surprise. He'd been in and out of the hospital over the course of nearly two years. We prayed! Oh my, how we had prayed for him to get better. But he didn't, not on our terms.

I went to school on the first Friday of a new semester thinking about all of the things you have on your mind when you're on your way to educate young people. Our house had been buzzing with the busyness of a typical morning when you have an army of children—or even only four. Everybody went about their business.

We'd been keeping continuous updates going through our family text group because Michael meant so much to us. Everyone was on the same page, at the same time.

I was halfway through a lecture when my phone buzzed. My wife doesn't usually text me in the middle of class. Mostly because she is typically in the middle of teaching her class at the same time. So I knew it was important.

"Excuse me a moment," I announced to my class as I picked up the phone from my desk. I flicked it awake with the gesture that's become second nature to all of us with an iPhone.

The soft glowing screen shared only three words, "his heart stopped." And then those little bubbles appeared letting me know there was more on the way, "pray".

I excused myself from the room and stepped into the hall to do just that. As I prayed I texted my friends. We share a large text group full of guys who pastor churches in our area. All of them are praying people. Even better, they are my friends. Friends are the first ones you seek when you need help.

Within a matter of moments heaven was hearing the name of my dear nephew from every corner of Arkansas. I was uncertain, and hopeful. And then four more words lit up my phone, "he didn't make it." I sat down in the hall outside of my classroom and cried.

When a loss like that lands it never lands softly. It shows up and changes everything. There is your life before and your life after.

RECORDS

In the days leading up to that Friday I was assailed by hard questions. None of them were new to me. I'd been helping people seek answers to those same questions for years. *Why did God do this? How can a good God let this happen? How am I supposed to feel right now? What should I do next?*

Usually, I'm the guy standing by the hospital bed helping people seek comfort. I don't do it because it's my job. Or even because I like it. There's a part of it that is terrible all the way through. I do it because at the very center of who I am I believe everyday with Jesus is better than any day without him. I do it because on the terrible days I think it's twice as true.

Over the course of the past year we'd had a string of really difficult conversations and some terrible days. The year before over the course of a few days Jamie's cousin had died, my dad's close friend had died, and my precious Uncle David had died. In the spring my loving grandma died. Death had become a begrudging acquaintance. I was sick of him. And then that Friday came.

I felt numb inside. Part of me hurt for all of the people I loved who were hurting. Part of me didn't know what to do about it.

I still don't know what to do about something like that. I never have. Yes, I'm a pastor. People seek me out in the middle of tragic circumstances frequently. And, I never know what to do. I think it's because you can't really do anything.

So what do we do? How should we feel? Because grief is a powerful force that is impossible to ignore. Talk is cheap on hard days.

It's easy to keep score concerning the things that don't seem to go your way. Sure, some people keep score about the little things. If they don't get their way with something inconsequential, or if someone behaves in a manner contrary to their wishes. But we all keep score when it comes to the big stuff.

What do you do when you have prayed, and prayed, and prayed for someone and then they die anyways? No one forgets that. The last thing I feel like doing in those moments is opening a bible or putting a worship song on.

Jesus' friend Paul made a profound statement about love that always comes to mind when I'm grieving. If you've been to a wedding you've probably heard it. A lot of married people I know begin their lives together by having someone like me read these words at their wedding. There's a lot of good stuff there, but one in particular always sticks out to me in sad times, "love keeps no record of wrongs." The irony isn't lost on me that part of what we read as couples begin their life together becomes so important in moments when a life is lost.

Love keeps no record of wrongs. What are we supposed to do with that? It sounds impossible. How could you forget when you feel like someone has let you down? Especially if that someone is supposed to be someone who loves you.

Sitting on the floor just outside my classroom on that Friday I felt like I had a long list of wrongs I was holding on to. I felt robbed. It didn't seem right for my young nephew's life to be cut so short. For that matter it didn't seem right for my grandma, my uncle, Jamie's cousin, or my dad's friend either.

It seemed like grief wasn't just an acquaintance I'd learned to accept. It seemed like death was a bad record being spun up again and again—on repeat. It felt wrong.

FOG

I carried all of that around for months. A kind of sadness had seeped in. One touched by the loss of people I loved. And then one Monday morning I found myself standing at the edge of a cliff overlooking the Arkansas River Valley I love so much.

I go up to the mountain top frequently. It's named after a place Moses visited in the Bible, Mount Nebo. After all the adventures Moses had with God his final adventure was on Mount Nebo. There at the top of Mount Nebo God pulled back the curtain on eighty years of promises. He showed Moses what was next for all of the people he had loved and led so well for so long.

Standing on my Mount Nebo I looked down across the valley and wondered about what was next. I looked at the way the early morning light struck from the East as it reflected across the river far below. I watched as a herd of deer ran across a meadow. I soaked in the morning sun, took long deep breaths of the crisp mountain air, and looked out. That's when it hit home.

Just across the valley stood another mountain. I've seen it hundreds of times. Probably thousands of times. It's called Spring Mountain. My dad used to tell me all kinds of stories about my grandpa's adventures on Spring Mountain.

I stood on Mount Nebo looking out across the expanse toward Spring Mountain, but I couldn't see it. Not because it wasn't there, but because something was in the way. In the moments before the sun had claimed the valley the fog stood thick.

Mountains don't just go away. There was no part of me that doubted the mountain was there. Yet, I couldn't see it. It was foggy.

That's when I realized how I see Jesus when grief is near. I can't see him. I can't get clear about it. I don't know what he wants for me. I don't know what he wants from me. It's just foggy.

My prayers seem to hit the fog and become lost. "What will the answer really be?" I often wonder.

The fog gets thick when you're hoping for a specific outcome and reality is something altogether different. If you're holding on to a record of wrongs it can get so much thicker. But Jesus isn't just there for us on the good days. Why? Because *everyday* with Jesus is better than any day without him. Not just the good ones.

On the days when the fog seems the thickest is when we need to remember. Yes, he is there. Yes, he is good. Yes, he loves you with an everlasting love.

No, he hasn't forgotten you. No, your prayers are not ignored. No, Jesus hasn't left you.

Jesus is God with us. He is with us. That's so important. Let's read it together one more time. Jesus is God with us. He is with us.

He is always there. When you can't see him—he's there. When you can't hear him—he's there. If you can't sense him, Jesus is there. Even when you can't understand. He is still there. He is God with us. Everyday.

Of course that doesn't mean we're only going to have good days. Life will never be perfect apart from heaven. I don't like it when life reminds me. But even on the bad days, weeks, or months, Jesus is there. Everyday with Jesus is better than any day without him.

CHAPTER 15
FORTY EIGHT HOURS

ANSWERS

My friend Hank is a pretty remarkable singer. Pretty much every week you can find him in a church helping people connect with Jesus through the songs he sings. I've known Hank for a while and it's been cool to watch him grow in his gift while also watching him become a family man.

Because Hank is my friend we speak regularly. He's one of those guys that I am privileged to run my race with. Hank is all in when it comes to Jesus. He knows everyday with Jesus is better than any day without him.

One day when Hank was on stage singing in front of a ton of people he reached for a high note in a song and missed it. For the first time his incredible talent didn't live up to its reputation. Hank was disappointed in himself, but wrote it off. Everybody makes mistakes.

And then it happened again. And then again. Hank became concerned.

He did what anyone should do, he sought help. Hank went to a doctor to find out what was wrong with his voice. Instead of helping him the doctor filled his head with a bunch of worrisome thoughts about potential problems. He left that appointment not only with less answers, but with full of scary ideas about what could be wrong. What was intended to help, had actually made him incredibly concerned for his future.

What's so cool about Hank is that he's not just a singer. During the week when he's not at a church encouraging people, he's in an office encouraging people. He spends his weekends rocking a guitar and his weekdays rocking a notebook. Hank is good at both. People show up to hear his voice from the stage because it encourages them to face their everyday problems with Jesus. And, people show up in his office during the week to hear his voice from his office chair because he encourages them to face their everyday problems with Jesus. No matter where you find Hank, his voice is one that points people toward Jesus.

Do you know why the first doctor couldn't help him? Vocal cords weren't his specialty. So, that doctor sent him to a new doctor that knew all there was to know about vocal cords.

On the day of his appointment I texted Hank to let him know I was praying for him. I wanted him to remember that his friends were cheering him on in his pursuit of answers. He got the answers he was looking for.

Forty eight hours made a big difference when it came to Hank's voice. He went from anxious uncertainty to clarity. And he did it with the help of just one voice. Why? Because when the right voice speaks over you, it makes a difference.

Hank found the right voice. It made a big difference. Now his voice continues to make a big difference from day-to-day and week-to-week.

QUESTIONS

One of my favorite things to do over the years has been to answer questions people have about God. Some guys do this and it becomes almost like a science or debate for them. More than a few guys I've heard do this bring a lot of theology, history, and knowledge of ancient languages to the table.

Take my friend Calvin for example. We have become great friends over the years. We both love to answer people's questions, but we do it in very different ways. When Calvin answers your question you can pretty much bet that at some point he's going to talk about a Greek word. Why does he do that? Because understanding old languages helps him understand what Jesus wants him to know today. And, because Calvin loves people, he loves to share what he knows with the ones who ask.

I also love to answer people's questions, but I'm no

theologian, scientist, or linguistic scholar. When I answer questions I just want to do one thing, I want to bring the right voice to someone searching for Jesus.

Without fail, almost every question that comes my way can be boiled down to one; what does God want for me? To give you an idea of the questions people send me from all over the world here is a list of some of the questions I got in the span of just two days:

How can I save my friend?

How can I get out from under this spirit of fear?

How can I find God's plan for my life?

I lost all my friends when I turned to Jesus. What do I do now?

Do I put God before my family?

How do I feel worthy?

What happens if someone we love doesn't go to heaven?

How do I deal with bad influences?

Can you pray for me?

I'm hearing a voice and I don't know if it's God or the devil. Can you help?

Do you think God still likes me?

Why would God ever want to talk to me?

Does God still love me?

Every time I read the questions I'm a bit humbled and a little more energized. Sometimes they leave me almost breathless from the desperation I can sense behind the words.

You can be sure of one thing. Jesus wants the people who are searching for his answers to find them. While there may be some mysteries reserved for the Halls of Heaven—things we'll only know on the other side of love's far horizon—Jesus isn't leaving your relationship with him up to guesswork.

When we show up to Jesus with our questions he doesn't spin the situation like some politician at a debate. He doesn't fill our heads or our hearts with the problems our question might cause. Instead, he points us toward a voice we can trust.

SEARCHING

Unfortunately, what seems far too common is people show up expecting to get what they need from Jesus only to be met by his stingy friends. I see this when someone brings their question to Jesus and, instead of getting answers, they are met by angry voices. I hear it when someone searching for Jesus questions the Bible, or Church, or our pet Christian ideas. It happens online, in our auditoriums, and at dinner tables.

There are a lot of people I've met who really like Jesus, but they don't like "going to church" very much. Do you know why? They showed up with questions and left with emotional bullet holes.

What do we call the room in a church building where people are supposed to meet with Jesus? It is a sanctuary. But is it? When searching people go looking for Jesus shouldn't it be his friends who are the first to point the way?

Instead of finding a voice they can trust they are all too often met with someone filling their heads and hearts with all of the scary problems their questions bring to mind. They don't need our fancy answers. They don't want the carefully articulated act someone in a committee has been planning all week.

They show up with questions. They show up searching. They want the only thing that can satisfy them, even though they often have no idea what that is. When they bring their questions to Jesus shouldn't they leave having been heard?

This is where you come in. Me, too. Those of us who know everyday with Jesus is better than any day without him should be the ones ready to listen. Jesus has already given us what we need.

That doesn't mean you'll never have questions of your own. It just means there are more than enough answers. When a teenager asks "how do I help my friend who is about to kill themselves?" There is an answer for that. For God's sake, help them! And when you ask, "God, why did this have to happen to my loved one?" There is an answer for that, too. Both are found in the hands of Jesus.

Let's get our stingy speeches, unwarranted arguments, and pet politics out of Jesus' way. He has what searching people need. He has what searching people want. He also has someone who can help—you. There is a generation searching for the heart of God. They're a generation desperate for a voice they can trust. Let's make sure they hear him instead of our opinions.

I don't think I'm the best voice. I do know I'm someone being asked. I don't know if my answers are always eloquent. I don't care if people agree with me. And I'm certainly not going in search of the approval of stingy people. All I know is when someone searching shows up I want to be a guy with a voice they can trust. I don't want to do it to feel good. I don't want to only do it when it is convenient. I want to do it everyday. Why? Because I know everyday with Jesus is better than any day without him. If you know it too, commit to helping searching people find their way to Jesus.

CHAPTER 16
HOME

TOGETHER

I love walking into my home after I've been gone for a bit. Whether it's a meeting across town, a speaking event in another city, or just an errand that calls me away for a few minutes—walking into my home is always good. Because home is where my family is.

We have four kids, Ethan, Jonathan, Matthew, and Anna. When I show up they get excited about it. I usually hear a chorus of "Daddy!" exclaimed from whatever corner of the house they happen to be in. Often I begin to hear it chanted before I even get up the stairs. It's good to be loved. It's even better to be loved by those who mean so much to you.

What I really love about my family is how they respond to anyone who shows up. The shouts of "Daddy!" are sometimes replaced by "Mommy!" or "Grandma!" or "Sarah!". My kids get excited when someone they love walks through our door. Everyday someone shows up they get excited.

It's not just adults they get excited about either. When my sons show up, their sister gets really excited. She will squeal, jump, and sometimes even cry happy tears that her brothers have come home. Each of them are the same way. If one has been gone, the rest cannot wait to have them nearby again.

We've managed to build a home where our family enjoys being together. I hope it's something that never changes because it makes all the difference in the world. We know we're not the same if we're not together.

Does that mean we spend twenty four hours a day together. No, that would be nuts. Actually, it did drive me a little nuts when the Covid-19 pandemic showed up a few years ago, but you already read that chapter.

While we are not literally with each other every second of the day—we know that we will always belong together. It's knowing where we belong that drives us to be together.

Plenty of you reading this get that. Your family is the same. Your family reacts in equally loving and endearing ways, even if they are unique to you.

What we all know is that building a place where belonging together takes on such an air of importance is not easy. It's not cheap. There's a cost. And it's not just a one time cost. It's an everyday commitment.

I'm not just talking about the jobs you have in order to pay for things like drywall, bricks, and electricity.

Those are costly, too. But there's another cost, a bigger and more pervasive cost than a mortgage.

To have a house you usually have to pay a mortgage. To have a home you have to put your heart into it. Lots of people have houses. Way too many people are up to their eyeballs in debt trying to pay for them. We went a different route when we got our house, but we're all in when it comes to making it a home. Jamie and I decided a long time ago we are willing to spend whatever it takes to make home a place where our family always knows they belong.

WANDER

I love Jesus' stories. I spend everyday with Jesus thinking about his stories. One of his best stories was about a home. Like any good home the kids were taken care of. The dad was good to his sons. They seemed to have all they could ever need. They were together.

But then something happened. One of the sons, the youngest one, decided to take off on his own. He was going to leave where he belonged. He was going to go out into the world and stake his claim.

Every young man and woman needs their shot at making their own way in the world. The struggle is good for them. Testing what they have inside is good for them.

Jesus' story was a bit different than that. The younger brother didn't just take off one day. He made some demands. He wanted to take his inheritance with him.

The father in the story loved his son. So he gave him his inheritance. The son was asking for something he would not have until after his father died. It was like he said, "I want your stuff, but I don't want you." Or, "I want your belongings, but I no longer belong here."

As a dad I could never really understand the next part of the story. The father gave the son everything he wanted and sent him on his way. There's not a scenario I can imagine where I could let my son go. Not because I don't want them to someday test themselves. I will spend the next several years preparing them for precisely that. I just can't imagine letting my boy walk away if I really thought he never planned to return.

I'm sure the father in the story didn't want that either. Maybe he just wanted his son to learn what it meant to really belong. I think he wanted him to learn the difference between being somewhere and belonging somewhere. I think he was hoping his son would learn the difference between a house and a home.

As the story goes the son took all of his stuff, told his family "adios", and hit the road. He was rolling big. He had wealth like he'd never dreamt of. What had been his dad's was his. He called the shots. He did whatever he wanted to do, whenever he wanted to do it. He spent what he wanted too, and pretty soon it was all gone.

Seriously, the younger son blew through his entire inheritance in some kind of record breaking speed. He spent money faster than a room full of politicians with your credit card. And when the money ran out he was stuck.

He had no money. He had no home. He had no family. And, he had no food. So, he had to get a job, but it was a pretty miserable job. He had to work feeding pigs. Even worse, he had nothing to eat except for what he was supposed to feed the pigs. Take it from someone who's fed pigs. That is nasty.

The son didn't know how lost he was, not yet. I don't know how long it took for him to reach his conclusion. But one second was too long with his head in the pig trough. Sitting there one miserable morning between Master Bacon and Lord Ham with some pig slop still on his shirt he finally realized how messed up his life had become.

He was eating nastiness in the pig pen, but not too far away was his father's house. All he had to do was return. He finally admitted his choices had taken him where he did not belong, and he resolved to go back—even if it meant returning as a slave instead of a son.

Jesus didn't say the son ran home, but how could you not if you knew home was waiting. My favorite part of the story is what the father did. He saw his son coming from a long way away. Why? Because he was looking for him. It's the part of the story that's too easy to miss. A good dad is always watching for those coming home.

When the lost son came back the father didn't tap his foot in indignation until the boy stood before him. He raced to meet him. Why? Because someone he thought dead showed up in the driveway. Someone he thought was gone was back. Someone he loved more than anything was where he belonged again.

The dad threw a party. A feast of epic proportions. Why? Because that's what you do when someone who was lost is found again.

The dad didn't lose his son. The son lost himself. But all it took to be found again was to go back to where he belonged.

When the older brother came home from work and found out about what was happening he threw a fit. He was outraged. Because the brother had left, had a wild time, and was welcomed again upon return. It didn't seem fair to the older brother. But mostly it was just jealousy. The older brother wanted his father to throw him a party, too.

The younger brother came home expecting to become a slave. He didn't think he belonged in the family as a son, so he thought he could just work hard enough to stay around. He thought he could earn a spot on the property by doing enough of the right things.

The older brother thought he was better than his brother. He didn't want to welcome him home. He wanted to remind him how lost he had been. He wanted to throw his mistakes in his face. He wanted to make the party about him. He thought he deserved the party instead of his little brother because he had done enough of the right things.

The father in Jesus' story corrected both his sons.

Both of them were wrong. So he did what a great father does.

To the younger brother he swapped out his rags for the good stuff. He put a ring on his finger that told everyone who's son he was. He restored him to the family in front of everyone. He held his son close.

To the older brother he reminded him how close to the father he had always been. He pointed out what the son enjoyed because of where he belonged. He told him all over again what it meant to belong to the family. He asked him to join the party.

The younger brother went to the feast with his dad. A chorus of shouting must have risen up. Because that's what is supposed to happen when you arrive where you belong. The older brother stood outside and sulked. He missed the party. All because he resented what the father was willing to do for his son who came home.

LOST

One Saturday afternoon I was grilling in the backyard while my two boys played downstairs. When dinner was almost ready I called down, "boys come up for dinner!"

Ethan, my oldest, replied with words that completely freaked me out, "Daddy, Jon is not down here."

"*What*?!" My heart jumped a little.

I'm pretty sure every parent has experienced this exact moment at some point. You momentarily lose sight of them in a crowd, or store, or perhaps they miss curfew. The *What Moment* we all experience as parents is the pain of suddenly realizing your loved one is not where they were supposed to be.

I wheeled into action but couldn't find my two year old. I called out to him. "Jon! Jon! Where are you buddy!?!" I called out again and again. Our neighbors started helping when they heard our shouts. Every nightmare scenario from all of the good Liam Neeson movies started replaying in my head. Nothing. Where was my son? I kept calling out.

Jamie was literally running laps around our neighborhood crying out for him like only a worried mother can. I frantically searched every room in our house as three excruciating minutes turned into thirty. Jon was lost, but I was losing it.

"He's nowhere." I remember thinking. Whatever that means? I went outside for about the tenth time to see if he had gone into the yard. Nothing. My neighbor had begun combing the woods behind our house.

One sudden and unexpected realization had tossed our world on its head. If that sounds dramatic it's because it certainly seemed that way. Jon was lost.

Ethan was crying. I was crying. Jamie was crying. Even while we all searched.

Honestly, at that moment it felt pretty hopeless. I just didn't know what could have happened or how it could have happened. I sat down on the floor in the middle of the living room and felt empty. So I said a very simple prayer, "God help me find my boy." I slowly climbed back to my feet, sick at my stomach, and started walking back through each room again in turn.

I don't know where the idea came from. Maybe it was God. Maybe it was desperation. But I walked into the spare bedroom downstairs. A room I'm certain I'd already looked in twenty times. I picked up an old unused curtain lying on a stack of boxes, and there he was. My boy. Jon was curled up under a curtain asleep on top of an unpacked box.

I scooped him up as I was shouting, screaming, and laughing all at the same time. I told Jamie, "I got him!" I told the neighbors, "I got him!" Ryan next door shouted "Hallelujah!"

We held him so close and he had no idea why. He just knew he woke up loved. He woke up in my arms.

There are people in your life who are lost. They don't even know they are lost. They are oblivious to it. They don't know the Father is watching. They don't know the Father is looking for them. They don't know the Father is waiting for them to come home.

They don't need those of us who follow Jesus to tell them how lost they are. They need us to look for them. People who know everyday with Jesus is better than any day without him should be the ones who always want lost sons and daughters to return home.

In the midst of my frantic searching Ethan didn't hide in a corner and sob. He was running through the house with all the energy of a five year old boy scared for his little brother. He was screaming, "JonJon! JonJon!" And unlike Jesus' story of the returned son, my Ethan didn't resent his brother when he was returned to us. Hot tears of fear turned to rejoicing.

Just like in Jesus' story we had a barbecue. We celebrated a little more that night. Our love grew just a little bit more. Why? Because what was lost was found.

When the one you love is lost to you it is frightening. You feel powerless to help. But we can't stop searching. Because they're never as far away as you may fear they are. They may just need you to come looking one more time.

When they are found, don't explain how lost they were. Celebrate how loved they are. Heaven smiles with all the warmth of a Good Father when the lost are found and love has the last word.

Everyday with Jesus is better than any day without him. The ones who really get it are the ones who want everyone else to get it, too. They don't complain about how lost people are. They just want them to know they are welcomed home.

CHAPTER 17
DELIGHT

FIRST

Behind the wheel I was holding on for dear life as we raced down an old country road. Dad held the wheel too as I sat in his lap. After all, I was only four years old. He put his foot on the gas and sent us hurtling forward. We weaved all over the road. I was driving —sort of.

Believe it or not this wasn't my first time driving a car. But the last time hadn't ended well. I wrote about it in *Learn Love Live*.

I had to hear about my first attempt behind the wheel from my family because I was too young to remember it. But I remember that moment on an old country road with my dad clearly. Why? Because I remember how much my dad loved me.

It's the first memory I have of love. I know it's not

the first moment I experienced it. Everyday of my life up to that one was jam packed with people who loved me. But that day on the dirt road in my father's lap holding on to the steering wheel was the moment I learned what it felt like to be loved.

When was the first time you remember feeling loved? Is it the hazy memory of a warm embrace from childhood? Maybe it was the look in your mother's eye on a Saturday morning. Perhaps a grandparent held you tight and whispered the words everyone should hear as often as possible, "I love you."

Maybe you found your way to this book, but your childhood wasn't great. If you spent your formative years dealing with pain and uncertainty "I love you" might not have meant much to you. At least, not until you grew to understand the power of those words when whispered by someone who really meant them.

The story of how we learn the meaning behind "I love you" is unique to each of us. For some it began as a rallying cry of affection and belonging. Some tragically experienced it as a bitter means to a cruel and selfish end. Usually at the hands of someone who exploited them.

My family loved me. They still love me. My days and memories are layered in love because of how much I knew it growing up. Love became a foundation for everything. Love became the ink my story was written in. It was the foundation each and every moment had to be fit into. One day at a time.

I know my story is my own. Yours is your own. Our stories are different. I don't know your story, but you have one.

The way love showed up in my life prevalent and powerful pointed me toward Jesus really early. By the time I prayed about it in the end zone of a football field in 1992 I was already old friends with Jesus. But that was the moment when I decided spending everyday with Jesus was something I wanted to do on purpose.

My story came with a lot of twists and turns after that day on the football field. All of my life's biggest mistakes happened after that day. Terrible things were done to me by some who pretended to love. And I did terrible things to people I should have loved. Both are part of my story.

We all have parts of our stories we don't like. There were things you did and there were things done to you. Neither are who you are. Not when you're spending everyday with Jesus. The things you did and the things done to you are not who you are.

Who are you? You are a child of God. Loved by him. You are someone God has always hoped to spend everyday with. Why? Because God delights in you.

ANNOUNCEMENTS

There's an amazing story in the bible about when Jesus was baptized. There was no tank full of warm water in a church building, just a dirty river. The day Jesus was baptized there wasn't a band playing music, but there was a heavenly host standing in awe. There were a bunch of people watching, too. I can't know for sure, but I bet most of them had no idea what was really happening.

John the Baptizer, the guy who baptized everyone back then baptized Jesus, too. If it sounds weird to you that some regular guy would baptize the son of God John felt the same way about it. He wanted Jesus to baptize him. John understood who Jesus was even when no one else did. Jesus insisted John do the baptizing, because it was meant to be that way. I think it's because Jesus knew what was about to happen.

The moment Jesus came up out of the water something incredible happened. I don't know what it looked like. I don't know what it felt like. But the guy who took notes and later shared them in the Bible nailed what it sounded like. In that moment when Jesus was baptized it sounded like a loving father telling everyone exactly how he felt about his son, "This is my Son, chosen and marked by my love, delight of my life." God told everyone in no uncertain terms that he delighted in Jesus.

If you know the rest of Jesus' story you know there were a bunch of religious guys there that day. They had spent a long time hassling John. John was doing his best to show people what it looked like to spend everyday with Jesus before anyone even knew who Jesus was. John kept telling them, "I'm here to get you ready." But the religious guys just wanted to heckle John.

When Jesus showed up the religious guys shifted their attention. The one John had been excited about had arrived. Everyone there had heard heaven's announcement. So why didn't they get excited about it too?

The religious guys were supposed to be the ones God worked through to help people. But they had it all wrong. They were supposed to be waiting for Jesus so they could tell everybody how great it would be to spend everyday with him. Instead they were busy telling everyone about themselves, their rules, and their inflated price for a sacrifice that no longer mattered.

God's announcement on the banks of the muddy river changed everything. Jesus was God's son. Jesus was loved by God. The Son of God had arrived.

The religious guys were forced to make a choice, but the truth is they had made their choice a long time ago. They had forgotten what it meant to be loved by a good father. They had forgotten what it meant to be loved by the Good Father. Instead, they had chosen what it meant to love themselves, their rules, and all of the ways they had complicated God's love for their neighbors.

That day on the side of the river God saw all of the religious dudes standing in line. And he passed them by. They had already had their shot. The Father showed up to demonstrate what a father is willing to do when he loves his son.

Religious people like their lines. They made everyone wait in lines. The people had to wait in lines to buy sacrifices. The people had to wait in lines to pray. There were always lines making people wait wherever the religious guys were in charge.

One of the first things Jesus taught us was what it looks like to walk past the lines. Why? Because God's love is big enough for everyone to hang onto at the same time. No one has to take turns. There are no lines.

Jesus walked past the religious people and their lines. He went right to the spot where the Father was waiting. John did what he was sent to do. Heaven rejoiced. The announcement was made. Jesus walked away from the river stamped by the Father's love, and everyone who was paying attention knew it. What an announcement God had made.

The religious people stayed mad about it right up until the moment they had Jesus murdered. And then they kept being mad about it. In fact, religious people are still mad about it.

What are they so mad about? Religious people get mad when Jesus doesn't wait in their line. Religious people get mad at anyone who doesn't ask their permission. They hated Jesus because he never wanted their permission. They hated Jesus because he spent everyday rejecting their lines. They hated Jesus because the ones who spent everyday with Jesus learned how much better Jesus was than any day standing in some religious guy's line.

CUT IN LINE

I'm a dad. Sometimes I even think I'm a good dad. We feed them. Buy them clothes and toys. The whole deal. And we only tie them up and lock them in the basement when they do something *really bad*. I'm kidding about that. We stopped doing that when our niece moved in. I really am joking about that. In fact, my kids seem to really like me as their dad.

Everyday I pick up the oldest two from school. We spent last year trying homeschool, but my wife didn't like one of the teachers so we sent them back to public school. This year I had to learn a hack because I hate the pick up line. I refuse to wait for an hour in a line to pick up my kids.

I walked in on the first day to get my boys, and they were like, "You can't have your kids."

I said, "You're going to give me kids."

They said, "You have to go get in line."

I said, "You're going to give me kids." (I know. I know. I sound like a jerk so far.)

The principal came out and asked, "is there a problem?"

I said, "I. Need. You. To. Give. Me. My. Kids."

He replied, "I'll work with you."

Here's where the hack comes in. I started driving up everyday at 3:05 PM. The bell for the kids walking home rings at 3:10 PM and my boys come out with them. I'm right there waiting. They get in my car. And we drive off. I skip the pick up line everyday. Guess what? All the parents watching that happen everyday probably hate me—but my kids love me.

Here's the point. God isn't waiting for permission when it comes to you. It doesn't matter who's watching. It doesn't matter if it upsets someone. God is ready for you!

The truth is, God is waiting for you. He's been waiting for you for a while now. He's waiting for you to walk out of whatever mess you've been in. He's waiting for you to leave behind the stuff that hasn't been working. He's ready for you to ditch the line! He's ready for you to stop seeking the approval of everyone else. He's ready for you to make a bee-line for the front door. He's waiting for you! Why? Because he knows what he wants you to know, that everyday with Jesus is better than any day without him.

Sometimes after I pick up the kids I'll take them for a snack. I don't take them to the bar. I wouldn't even know where to find one. I take them to get something I know they'll like. Even though sometimes I'll act like I'm taking them somewhere terrible just to mess with them.

Sometimes I'll ask if they want to go get some shots. Not those kinds of shots! I don't even know where the bar is. Sometimes I'll ask if they want to go to the dentist. Except that doesn't always work because Jon likes the dentist. We're praying for him.

No. I like to be with my kids. I enjoy being together,

everyday. So I like to lean over in the car and whisper a simple question. Do you know what I like to ask? Where do you want to go?

Here's what I know about God. He's the best dad. No matter what you've been through or are going through He's leaning down over your life and whispering, "Where do you want to go?

When a guy named Paul needed to write a letter to his friends in Rome they talked a lot about where everyday with Jesus was taking them. Paul was tired of seeing the people he loved just going for laps around the same old problems all the time.

He wanted them to leave behind the expectations of those around them. Paul was hoping they would take living everyday with Jesus to heart. He was full of good advice for them. He spelled out so many of the details about how to live for God and what life with Jesus could be like for his friends.

Paul's advice to his friends wasn't very complicated. He said they should stop conforming to the same pattern of the people around them. He was telling them that everyday with Jesus is not only better than any day without him but it's also different, too.

Instead, he offered, they could be transformed by renewing their mind. This wasn't like changing their minds over and over again. It was way better. Renewing just means making it new all over again. Only Jesus can do that.

Paul went on to promise his friends that if they did

the first two parts then they would be able to actually test what God wanted for their life. And, not only that, but he said they would even be able to approve what God wanted for their lives. That's pretty remarkable if you think about it.

I've known a lot of people over the years who got way off track trying to figure out what God wanted them to do with their lives. When all the while God was simply saying, "Spend everyday with Jesus and you get to decide."

It's not rocket science. It's not complicated. We're supposed to stop doing life like everyone else. Jesus wants those of us spending our days with him to move the measuring stick. What works for the people who aren't rolling with Jesus doesn't work for us anymore, because it never really worked at all.

We leave behind our old measure for success. And it causes transformation. It's a perspective shift. It's leaving behind the way we saw it before we invited Jesus to show us a new and better way to live.

The act of leaving behind what doesn't work, and the broken patterns it creates in our lives will cause us to step forward into something altogether different—something better. We will begin to live and breathe what God wants for us. This is often called "God's will" by people who follow Jesus. It's like a Christian code name for the purpose God has for you.

One of the promises Paul made was a description of God's purpose. Paul said God's purpose for you is good. It's meant to benefit you. He also said God's purpose for you is pleasing. In other words, you're going to like it—and so is He. Finally, Paul said, God's purpose for you is perfect. The purpose God has in store for you is the sweet spot where life gets really great. It's the place where you really begin to know everyday with Jesus is better than any day without him.

CHAPTER 18
BEATING TEMPTATION

DRAWN IN

Have you ever found yourself lured by the scent of leftover pizza in the fridge at midnight? Or maybe you've had that "buy one, get one 50% off" deal wink at you, even when you know your closet's already bursting at the seams. Temptation can be a sneaky thing! But temptation is more than pizza and weekend sales. It's gravity, pulling at us all the time!

Not too long ago I heard about an asteroid that was supposed to be heading for Earth. Did you hear about it? It was supposed to hit the U.S. in November. You might hear that and think this is a political joke, but I'm not kidding. Actually there was only a small chance it would even make landfall. Besides, the whole thing was only six feet in diameter–tiny by asteroid standards. I don't think we even needed to send Bruce Willis and

Ben Affleck. We probably could have just sent Steve Buscemi.

One of my favorite stories from the Bible is about Jesus being tempted. In the story he was tempted three times. This won't surprise you, but Jesus nailed it. He didn't succumb to the temptations. He overcame them. I bet this isn't a surprise to you either, but we don't always ace it. We screw up. We drop the ball. All of us.

Failing doesn't make you a failure. And just because you failed last time, doesn't mean you have to next time. No one enjoys the consequences of succumbing to the enticement of temptation. No one says "Sign me up!" when it comes to consequences. Usually because we aren't thinking about them.

What if we could see temptation coming? I believe we can. Jesus showed us what to expect. And if we know what to expect we can take measures to guard our hearts and our lives. I am so completely convinced we don't have to give in to our temptations.

BREAD

In Luke's account of the story Jesus was baptized and immediately did a wilderness retreat without the luxuries—no food, no room service, no s'mores. Satan, ever the opportunist, thought, "Ah! Jesus is hungry! Maybe I can bribe him with bread."

Jesus was quick on his feet even when he was hungry. He replied with a Bible verse from the Old Testament. Jesus said, "Man doesn't live just on bread alone." That's right, Satan. Carb-loading isn't everything! Jesus didn't mean you could sub in some Taco Bell or a good steak. He meant physical nourishment is not enough.

You can have a full belly and an empty life. You can have a full bank account and be empty. You can be surrounded by people and be lonely. We don't always know what we need.

It reminds me of the Israelites, who took God's miraculous manna for granted when they were wandering through the wilderness. Ever complained about daily blessings? The beautiful sunrise, the air we breathe, the coffee that miraculously appears in your cup every morning?

The Israelites frequently grumbled and complained about the bread from Heaven. Even miracles can seem mundane when they show up everyday. What kind of everyday miracle are you taking for granted? God provides what we need, but not just for our belly. Man does not live on bread alone!

Why did the enemy tempt Jesus with bread first? Because Jesus was hungry. Enticement always follows emptiness.

You will always be tempted where you are empty. If you are lacking intimacy, you will be tempted with lust. If you are lacking financially, you will be tempted with financial dishonesty. If you are lacking emotionally, you will be tempted with toxic relationships. If you are lacking spiritually, you will be tempted with false idols. You will *always* be tempted where you are empty. It doesn't mean you will *only* be tempted where you are empty. But the place where you are weak is where your enemy is coming for you.

It's hard to do the right thing when you are empty. If you're hungry, fatigued, anxious, afraid, angry, or doubtful–any of those things can sideline or surprise you. Are you trying to live off of the wrong thing? Life with Jesus holds the answers.

EGO

Imagine somewhere so high you could see all the kingdoms of the world in a moment. Talk about a bird's eye view. Satan took Jesus somewhere like that. Like some kind of ancient middle eastern Space-X. From there they saw all the known kingdoms of the world at a glance. It must have been something to behold.

What knocked my hat in the creek is the audacity of what the devil put on the table. He offered the whole world to Jesus. All, in exchange for worship. Imagine this: Satan, in his sneakiest salesperson voice, offering Jesus a deal. All kingdoms of the earth for a moment of worship.

Jesus' response was simple. An emphatic, definitive, "No." What Satan failed to note is that all the kingdoms of this world already belong to the King of kings.

What he tempted Jesus with didn't work, but here's where it works on us–our egos. Like thinking you're the lord of the dance floor after one dance lesson. Or posting that one salad on Instagram and declaring yourself a health guru. Before we know it, our ego has written checks our character can't cash.

Pride does come before a fall. Temptation follows ego. Where you're puffed up the most is where you'll trip up the most. No one likes scraped knees.

Jesus didn't have an ego. Why? He didn't come to be served, but to serve. He was constantly warning his friends about this. "Whoever would be first must be last...." Stuff like that. If we want to evade the temptation of our ego We have to make sure we aren't building a life centered around our own importance. Why? Because temptation follows ego.

OPPORTUNITIES

Jesus stopped temptation in its tracks twice. How? With scripture. So the devil decided to take a new angle. Satan quoted scripture to Jesus. What didn't work on Jesus sometimes works on us.

How often do we see people hurling around Scripture like Holy Hand Grenades in support of their opinions? How many times have you seen two Christians arguing about something? They each probably loaded up their arguments with Bible verses. Every time this happens, the enemy gets a leg up in the relationship. That is not the Jesus way.

The third temptation of Jesus was a weak one-two combination. The devil was trying to mess with his identity and his ability. He challenged Jesus to prove himself. The enemy attempted to question the very identity of Jesus. Not smart. Because Jesus' identity came with a crown and a kingdom. Even so, he gave his life away. He didn't live entitled.

Temptation follows entitlement. When you think you're owed something you'll start making excuses to get what you want. We see this in the headlines everyday.

Temptation always looks for the next opportunity. It's the sneaky right hook we often don't see coming. But we can be ready. We might stumble occasionally, maybe even take a hit or two. But if we spend everyday with Jesus we've got all we need in our corner.

We are never going to be perfect, but we can be ready. Because sin is a habit, temptation is a tricky kind of invitation. Cut it off at the knees by preempting bad habits with the kind that come from doing everyday with Jesus. Live satisfied in Jesus. Live close to Him. Live his purpose on purpose. Love the people in your path. Do it all in the service of others and your ego won't take center stage. Trust who you are as a child of God. We are entitled to nothing but given so much! Grace is amazing. Getting these things right is like throwing a wet blanket on the enemies' big plans for you. That's how you beat temptation. By spending everyday with Jesus.

CHAPTER 19
MAKE IT SIMPLE

RED LETTERS

When I first strutted into my dorm in the 90's (the era of glitter pants and beanie babies), I had one mission: be faithful to God. Sunday school was fantastic, don't get me wrong. But when the rubber met the road – or rather, when I stepped onto that dorm floor – I felt like a fish out of water. The world was wilder than Noah's Ark on karaoke night.

So I did something that made everyone who loved me nervous. I threw out almost everything I believed about everything. Any ideas that couldn't address what I was suddenly seeing everyday got thrown away—why? Because by then I had spent years reading my Bible every night. Somewhere between Genesis and Revelation, I had become completely convinced Jesus loved me and he wanted a relationship with me.

So, I threw away all of the man made stuff I'd

learned growing up. Out went the cobbled together Sunday school theology. It was passed down by well-meaning people that loved Jesus too; but they'd never experienced my new context. All of the rule based traditions that had seemed so important when my world was smaller got the boot, too. I made a clean slate.

You know how sometimes teachers give you feedback, you're left thinking, "Okay, is this a riddle?" Well, about the same time I reset my faith a teacher kept scribbling K-I-S-S at the top of all my papers. Now, I wasn't the brightest crayon in the box, but getting what I thought were love notes from my professor felt... weird. After weeks of my overactive imagination running wild, I confronted him. I was like, "Hey, are you suggesting we start a band or something?" After he stopped laughing – he enlightened me with that timeless acronym, "Keep It Simple, Stupid."

I've spent more than two decades trying to introduce people to Jesus. I have spent hour after hour reading the Bible, talking about the Bible with friends and strangers, and teaching the Bible to crowds of all sizes. Again and again I've encountered the same problem. So many people try so hard to know so much about the Bible they miss the one it's meant to introduce them to. They don't keep it simple.

The Bible was always meant to introduce you to Jesus. Why? You already know the answer. Because everyday with Jesus is better than any day without him.

The truth of that statement is so powerful we can't afford to waste one day in pursuit of overcomplicated religion. We all do it sometimes. When we do it's like trying to assemble IKEA furniture using quantum physics. We lean towards rules and religion when we get hung up on one another's behaviors. We move more towards religion when we want everyone to agree with our take on Jesus.

Why do we complicate things? Maybe it's human nature, or perhaps we've just had too much caffeine. We all love a good rule book, especially if it proves we're right and everyone else is slightly less right.

I love that some Bibles have Jesus' words in red. It's like a spiritual highlighter saying, "Hey, don't skip this part!" For me it's also an important reminder to keep it simple. Because the complicated stuff people came up with doesn't keep us in step with Jesus. It just moves us back toward our own agenda all over again. No wonder so many people seem to be going in circles.

When we do this I think Jesus himself is standing there waiting for us to come back to him. He sees us take another lap and is desperate to get our attention. He's holding up what we should have been reading all along—some red letters.

RESET

When I reset my faith I only kept two beliefs: Jesus is the Son of God and the Bible is the Word of God. I believed, stronger than a pot of cafeteria coffee, that the answers were in the Bible. I just had to roll up my sleeves and find them.

For the next two and a half years I combed through the pages. Every night my best friend and I would have wrestling on one TV, where dudes would be pretending to beat each other up, and a football game on another TV with guys actually beating each other up, as we talked about the Bible.

Eventually some other people started gathering with us. By the end of a year we had dozens of college guys cramming into a tiny dorm room that smelled like old pizza and gym socks.

I spent the next fifteen years doing the same thing. I'd find a group of college students interested in learning what the Bible could teach them and we'd do our best to learn it and live it together. There was really only one rule. Keep it simple. Actually, that wasn't even a rule—it was just how we rolled.

I've got a lot of buddies who do, but I've never liked Nascar. I totally get why they do. The big loud cars and skill it takes to drive an oversized Hotwheel at 250 miles per hour are pretty amazing. It's just too complicated for me. They just keep taking another lap. Remember, I like it simple.

I did go to the drag races once and found out that was more my speed. Do you know why? It's simple. They just go in a straight line. And when they get where they are going they stop.

If you've been struggling to really spend everyday with Jesus chances are you've overcomplicated it. Or maybe someone else in your life did. Stop taking laps. Jesus is beckoning you to move past the bloated ideas of men and step into a better life. Move straight for him into the kind of life where you actually walk everyday with him instead of someone else's opinion.

"Keep it simple" became my college anthem. Close runners-up included "Never trust cafeteria shrimp" and "Don't buy the book!"

Keeping it simple is so important. It's also really hard because getting it wrong feels right. I can't tell you how many times I've heard well meaning people explain the love Jesus has for us in overly complicated ways. We almost always try to overcomplicate it. It's our nature. How can something so good be so simple?

Luckily we don't have to figure that out. We don't have to make sense of how the cosmic affection of our great big amazing God can be boiled down to the simplicity of a carpenter giving his life for us. All because he wants us to know everyday with him is better than any day without him. We don't have to figure that out. Because Jesus did it for us. He took the circle people had been going around in for years and turned into a straight line. It took me way too long to figure this one out.

ON THE ROCKS

After college I spent my years helping college students walk with Jesus. I did a good job of keeping it simple most of the time. But inevitably religion and rules would creep their way back into my way of doing things. And then I went to Ecuador.

My buddy Jake had been trying to get me to go with him for so long that I half-expected him to start sending postcards signed "wish you were here!" I'd alway said no, but then one day I surprised us both and said yes instead. A few weeks later we were camped out on the edge of a cliff on the west coast of South America.

We would spend our mornings slinging mortar and piling bricks as we helped secure a local campground being built for kids. Because of the intense heat we'd get up really early and work through the morning. But shortly after lunch we'd call it quits in order to spend the hottest part of the day out of the blistering sun.

We were staying there for over a week so I found a new rhythm pretty quick. Each afternoon I would go down to the local market to buy an ice cream and a soda. I would carry it back to cliffs where we were staying and I would read my Bible.

The place where I chose to sit with my bible was about eighty feet above the water. The waves would roll in and thunder upon the rocks below with a steady cadence that felt like God's heart beating. The crashing waves would lift up from the bluegreen depths carried on the ocean breeze and break into a cool mist. It swept up and over the edge of the cliff where I sat reading.

I'd gone there to help my friend Jake help his friends. We were doing hard work everyday designed to help people get to know Jesus in a safe place. In the days since arriving I'd seen more poverty than I'd ever before imagined. I had also interacted with hundreds of local people eager to live everyday with Jesus. That's where my heart was the day I sat down on my cliff and read something I had read at least one hundred times before.

ALL

I read a story about a day when Jesus was doing what he does better than anyone. He was helping people. Only, some religious guys kept getting in the way.

Jesus wanted people to understand what he hopes you and I will grasp here and now. Following Jesus isn't complicated. Loving God was never meant to be complicated. In fact, it's incredibly simple.

It wasn't immediately complicated. It became more and more complicated over time. Until it was so complicated it stopped being about loving God at all. The guys who were in charge of helping regular people like you and me know God instead showed up everyday with their complicated set of instructions.

Sometimes the complicated religious guys would follow Jesus around. When he would make a statement about something profound like mercy or justice they would jump in to complicate things. One day they hammered Jesus with a long list of complicated questions. They even asked Jesus about taxes. It doesn't get any more complicated than taxes.

There's something important for you and I to remember. If we treat Jesus more like the tax code than a friend who really loves us—we're probably not really living everyday with Jesus. He wants you to ditch the tax code approach and just go with him. Everyday is better with him when you put down the complicated stuff and just take the next simple step.

The next question the tax code crowd asked Jesus was meant to be a deal breaker. It was a loaded question. After asking him easy stuff like the tax code they brought out the big guns. The question of all questions.

One of the religious guys asked Jesus, "what is the most important commandment?" This was a big deal because the Bible those guys used had hundreds of rules in it. It was complicated. Really complicated. To make matters worse over the years they had added all kinds of extra rules about the rules. They took something complicated and made it impossible.

Jesus answered them like only he could. Jesus did what Jesus does so well. He took something men had made complex, and he reminded them how simple it was supposed to be.

He redefined important for everyone listening, but he didn't do it by coming up with a flashy answer. He just reminded them of something Moses had told them hundreds of years earlier.

What did he tell them? Jesus told them the most important thing for them to do was to love God. It was always meant to be that simple. News flash—it still is. But, because Jesus doesn't leave people hanging he went on to explain what loving God really looked like. He didn't just tell them *what* to do. Jesus explained *how* to do it. And, yeah, it was really simple.

Jesus said loving God wasn't complicated. The way

we are supposed to love God according to Jesus is to engage all of our heart, soul, mind, and strength. That is not complicated, but we have to be honest with ourselves and admit it's not easy either.

Reading the story where Jesus simplified everything for the crowd simplified everything for me. It was the day I realized you don't need a fancy dictionary to understand the Bible. You don't need a list of extra books. You don't need to google every obscure little thing.

That was the day I realized the Bible isn't homework to be learned, it is a love letter to be lived. Jesus knew his contemporaries had over complicated things. So, when they asked him to make it simple he did, and we can apply the same thing to everyday life with Jesus.

CHAPTER 20
EVERYTHING

UNCOMPLICATED

A couple years ago my friend Tyler convinced me to start making videos for social media. His big idea was for me to do what I was already doing every Sunday at Church, but to make it shorter. I started doing my sermons in my empty living room every Monday morning. Yes, it felt as weird as it sounds. What happened next blew my mind. People started watching the videos. But not just a few people, like my mom and her friends. Hundreds of people. Thousands of people all over the world. It was crazy.

Now, it seems like everyday I get a question from someone somewhere that leaves me scratching my head. Part of me is really humbled and honored that I would be the guy someone wants to ask for help when it comes to their faith, but there's another part that sits there wondering how they even came up with the question.

People ask some really good questions sometimes. Stuff like, "what does it take to really follow Jesus?" I also get a lot of questions about sin. For some reason people want to ask me if doing certain things will make God mad at them.

I try to answer these questions with love and grace. I want to honor the question because I want to love the person who asked it. They aren't just a random string of odd usernames floating my way over the internet. They are a son or a daughter God loves.

On occasion I'll get a question that seems like it's coming from the tax code guys Jesus talked to. Those kinds of questions are usually pretty loaded. You can sense the heart behind them in the words they choose to use. Also, because their questions aren't always really questions. They are taking a position and trying to bait me into an argument by slapping a question mark on the end of it.

I used to be the kind of guy that would have loved to argue about it, but I grew up. I moved on. I came to understand just how completely unnecessary all the endless debates are. Debating serves our ego, not Jesus.

Now I leave the arguing to the ones who enjoy it. I want to invest my time and attention helping people who are more interested in Jesus than being right about everything. It is amazing how uncomplicated following Jesus is when you make it all about actually following him.

Jesus wanted his friends to know loving God is not complicated. Spending every day with him is not complicated. We shouldn't make it complicated. But what do we do all of the time? Yeah, we make it complicated.

The only time the Bible talks about Jesus getting irritated with people was when they made things complicated. When his friends tried to come up with complicated instructions for kids who wanted to see Jesus he got annoyed with them. When the people at a place called The Temple made worship complicated Jesus got so mad he threw everyone out. Jesus wanted people to rediscover the truth of a simple approach to God.

Jesus answered them like only he could. Jesus did what Jesus does so well. He took something men had made complex, and he reminded them how simple it was supposed to be. He told them God wants us to love him with all of our heart, soul, mind, and strength. It isn't always easy, but it's not complicated.

HEART

I hear people say this, or something like it all the time, "Follow your heart." The problem is that following your heart is terrible advice on its own. Your heart is not the best chauffeur. So don't put it behind the wheel of your life.

On the flipside I hear pastors like me telling people to ignore their feelings way too often. Stop telling people to ignore their feelings. It's not helpful. Feelings are helpful. You feel what you feel for a reason. God designed your body with feelings. Feelings are supposed to be there.

When Jesus told his friends to love God with all their heart he wasn't talking about an emotionless kind of love. There can be no love without emotion. Because real love involves feelings—we just have to remember it also involves more than feelings.

Your heart is the seat of your passions and desires. Your heart is where your deep inclinations come from. Not all of your instincts are bad. Once you start spending everyday with Jesus your heart changes. He wants to change your heart. Why? Because he wants to help you love God with your whole heart.

Instead of telling people not to trust their feelings, or not to make decisions using their feelings, it might be more helpful if we guided them toward a better way to feel. That's what Jesus did. He said we should engage our whole heart when loving God.

How? We should submit our passions to God. We should filter our dreams through what God wants for us. We should realize that as God's kids we can take our cues from the things that stir our heart. We don't need people out there running around following Jesus without engaging their hearts. There are more than enough pretenders acing that already. Jesus' friends should be the ones bringing all of their heart to the team. Which is exactly what Jesus said we should do. We were meant to love God with all of our hearts.

SOUL

What about your soul? How do you engage your soul when it comes to spending everyday with Jesus? It's important to think about because Jesus said it was part of how we love God. By doing it with all of our soul.

I've been to too many funerals lately. I hate funerals. If you've been to one you know they can be both bitter and sweet. They are bitter because it is so hard to say goodbye to someone you love. They are sweet because you know they have gone to the place where walking with Jesus can no longer be measured by a calendar.

A few months ago my grandma passed away. Along with my friend Kenny I was asked to officiate the funeral. Almost every funeral has one thing in common. The moment you pass by your dearly departed loved one and look upon their remains. As you look at the person who meant so much to you, there is likely a flood of emotions. But one thing has always stuck with me. The face you see belonged to them. It's the face you knew and loved. But when life is gone you can tell that something is missing.

That something that's missing is a soul. You can call it a spark. You can call it a force. There are many different ways people try to explain our soul.

I think the best explanation for our soul is found in what else is missing when we look down at our loved ones at a funeral. Breath is missing. Our soul is the breath of God that first made human life possible. The day God breathed into a mud ball in a rugged garden the human soul that was born is what made Adam a man.

So how do we love God with all of our soul? By loving him authentically. By opening yourself up to the most sincere, honest, and sometimes vulnerable places inside us. The Bible is full of moments like this from guys who loved God. King David wrote a bunch of Psalms called laments. They were sad. He shared them because he knew it was important to live everyday with God, not just the easy or good ones. Jeremiah wrote a short book in the bible literally called Lamentations. To you and I it just sounds like a bunch of confusing whining from a grown man. It's actually a powerful little book that lays out the deep soul work of God's friend.

David and Jeremiah both got it right when it came to loving God with all of their soul. It can be as simple as talking to him about your day—the good and the bad. But ultimately it just means we don't hold anything back.

ALL OF IT

When the lawyers showed up to challenge Jesus he gave them a simple answer, but it wasn't multiple choice like a pop quiz in college. We don't get to pick and choose. Choosing to love God with your heart, soul, mind, and strength isn't like picking out your favorite flavor of ice cream at Baskin Robbins. It's actually better because the choice was already made for you. You get every flavor when it comes to loving God.

Jesus wants us to go big when it comes to loving with our whole heart. He wants us to be real and love him out of a deep place of sincerity. He also wants us to love God with our minds–the whole thing.

Our minds aren't just repositories for random trivia or where we store all our passwords. They're powerful tools in our spiritual journeys. The mind is where we wrestle, discover, and most importantly, connect deeply with God's truths.

I've seen college dorm rooms tidier than my thoughts on some days. But in the midst of the mental clutter, there's an opportunity to uncover treasures. The kind that revives and strengthens our love for God.

Loving God with all our mind isn't just about absorbing Scripture like a sponge. It's about letting that truth seep out, influencing our choices, our actions, and our relationships. Like adding an unexpected ingredient to a dish and watching it transform into a gourmet delight.

Next time you find yourself in a moment of reflection, whether it's on a cliff, in your favorite chair, or while sneakily snagging that midnight cookie, remember to invite your mind to the party. Dive into God's Word. Ponder, question, and embrace. Because when we love God with all our mind, we're unlocking a depth of relationship that's richer than we can imagine.

When we love God with our entire mind, we're giving ourselves permission to see the world through a brand-new lens, a Jesus-tinted lens. It's like taking a regular photo and slapping on a filter that turns everything vibrant, meaningful, and downright beautiful. We start to perceive challenges not as mountains to be conquered, but as opportunities to grow and reflect His glory. Those mundane daily tasks? They become acts of worship when seen from a perspective of purpose and gratitude.

Think back to the last time you were on a ladder or went from sitting on the ground to standing on a chair. Suddenly, the vantage point changes and so does your perspective.

Similarly, loving God with our minds changes our point of view. We begin to rise above the pettiness, the mundane, and the limitations of routine. We begin to dream bigger, hope with unwavering faith, and find joy in places we never thought to look. This mental shift isn't just about increased knowledge or greater intellectual engagement with Scripture. It's about understanding the vastness of God's love and His intricate design for each one of us. It's recognizing that every challenge, every joy, every tear, and every hearty laugh is part of His grand narrative for our lives. And when our mindset aligns with His vision, the picture becomes clearer, and the journey, infinitely more rewarding.

Next time you feel bogged down, remember to shift your perspective. Look beyond, look deeper, and watch the world transform in His light. Everyday is an opportunity to walk arm in arm with Jesus as you love God with everything you've got.

CHAPTER 21
LIVE THE STORY

OLD GUITARS

Growing up I played basketball a lot. I was never good enough to bet my future on it, but there was a season when I was more passionate about playing basketball than everything else. I hurt my knee in back to back seasons during high school which sent me spiraling into depression. Noticing my distress, my cousin took an ancient guitar that had been sitting in an old shed for almost forty years and refurbished it for me.

If you're a guitar expert you'd take one look at my old guitar and instantly write it off as a piece of junk. And you wouldn't be wrong. But to me the guitar was significant. Because it was my avenue for learning a whole new world. The world of music.

What's interesting is that my dad already owned two guitars. You'd think I would have just learned to play one of his, right? Theoretically you'd be right–but my dad is left-handed while I'm right-handed. We could sit and play together, sharing melody filled moments as I learned how, but we could never share the same guitar.

A few months after I had started playing I was at my grandparents' house. By then the word was out–I was attempting to learn to play the guitar. It created a mild ripple in my family because my mom's cousin had been the legendary guitar player for none other than Johnny Cash. All of a sudden there were some weird and surprising expectations that seemed to pop up around me about something I didn't even know if I was good at.

One quiet afternoon, as I sat in my grandpa's living room, he asked me to play something for him. I told him I hadn't brought my guitar with me that day. With a mischievous twinkle in his eye, ever full of surprises, Grandpa winked and said, "wait right there." He disappeared into the back of the house, emerging a couple of minutes later holding a breathtaking guitar. Its deep black finish was punctuated by an orange, yellow, and red starburst on the front. Set into the heart of that burst of color was a pearl hummingbird. Grandpa handed me his guitar and said, "Son, play this." So I did.

Strumming it, I was transformed. For the first time, I felt like a real guitar player. Why? Crafted with precision, Grandpa's guitar was designed to belt out beautiful music when in the hands of someone who knew how to use it. It was simply incredible.

Until that moment I hadn't really had a chance to

know what I could do with what I was learning. Because my old guitar was pretty limited. But Grandpa's guitar was limitless. It could do anything as long as I knew how to do it. All I had to do was apply what I'd been learning.

JUST DO IT

How you apply what you've learned matters. You'll never know what you're capable of doing until you begin to do it. Jesus was the showcase when it comes to the art of loving people. He was constantly teaching his disciples. The catch? They had to be present, engaged, and eager to learn, but they had to take it one step further. Because what you learn undeniably matters, but how you begin to apply that knowledge matters even more.

Jesus' brother James wasn't his biggest fan during the part of Jesus' story we read in the four gospels. We could guess at a lot of reasons for why, but we'll never really know until we get a chance to ask him ourselves. After the resurrection James totally changed his tune. I guess seeing your dead brother you'd been giving a hard time running around again after you knew he'd died would do the trick.

Later James became a pastor of the young church in Jerusalem. In a short letter written to his friends James gave them a pretty stout challenge. He told them to be people who "do the word". At first glance this sounds like one of those social media challenges where people dare one another to display their faith. That's not what James' challenge meant at all.

James was tired of seeing people step into an everyday life with Jesus, but fail to do what Jesus said. I don't think he was mad at them about it. I think he knew firsthand what it was like to get it wrong. And, he was hoping they would find a better way to live. One where you don't just listen to the words of Jesus, but you actually obey the words of Jesus. In fact, James was pretty pointed about it. He said that when we don't apply what we've learned from Jesus we are actually being dishonest with ourselves.

The tough part about what James had to say is that it rings so true. We see people everywhere who talk a lot about Jesus but don't seem to be doing what he said.

Remember Nike? Of course you do. Ever since the 80's it's been everywhere. If you were a basketball player like I was you undoubtedly ran around in Nikes at some point. What was their slogan? I know you remember it. We all do. Because we heard it a million times growing up. *Just do it.*

James' charge to his friend is the Bible's charge for you and I to *just do it.* We can't stop short at only hearing the words of Jesus. It's not enough just to know it in our head. We have to be people who know it with our hands, our words, and our heart.

NEIGHBOR

When I was born my parents lived far away from my grandparents. Just in cast you didn't know, parenting without help is hard. My wife and I only began to understand this recently, but we've watched several of our friends struggle with it for years. And we've even seen some of them move hundreds of miles in order to change it.

My mom and dad knew the struggle firsthand. But some kindly neighbors showed up in their lives like angels from heaven. They did it in the biggest and best ways. They loved my parents heart and soul. And they proved it by showing up in strength and making it clear. They didn't only do it every once in a while either. It was everyday.

Every day the sun rises on another chance to go all in with Jesus. We get to decide. How are we going to live today? Are we going to love God with all of our heart? Are we going to love God with all of our mind? Are we going to love God with all of our soul? Are we going to love God with all of our strength?

That's what God wants for us. He wants us to know that every day with Jesus is better than any day without him. But because God loves us he doesn't stop at just what he wants us to know. He shows us how it's done. He came here and he did it himself in the form of his son. And then Jesus showed us how we could do it, too. So how do we do it? We love our neighbor as we love ourselves.

For some people loving their neighbor is the hardest thing Jesus told us to do. For others the really difficult part is the part where you're supposed to love yourself. But the instructions Jesus gave us are true for everyone. We love our neighbor as we love ourselves. Not when it feels good. Not when it's convenient. But always, every day. It's in loving our neighbor as ourselves daily that we truly begin to believe and experience how much every day with Jesus is better than any day without him.

Let's be honest. Holding up our Bibles and waving them around for a trend on TikTok is a lot easier than opening our Bibles and letting the instructions shape our lives. Especially when it comes to loving our neighbors.

Jesus' brother James took a lot of convincing. It wasn't until after Jesus rose from the dead that he joined the team. Seeing a brother rise from the dead after a bunch of bad guys poked holes in him would do the trick. James was later repeating the words of Jesus. He reminded his friends that loving your neighbor is how you prove you're really living the story God wants for you.

I get it. It's hard to love your neighbor when their dog barks all night and their friends keep parking in front of your driveway. It's hard to love your neighbor when their cat keeps using your tulips like a port-a-potty. Look, your neighbor may not vote like you, pray like you, or look like you. He may not even like you, but we still have to love our neighbor. Loving your neighbor is not just about nodding in agreement with the Bible; it's about actively searching for opportunities. It's about living out our instructions.

INSTRUCTIONS

One year I got a fancy new saw for my birthday. I was really excited because it was the final tool I needed in order to make something I'd been wanting to try for a while. I got the saw home, opened the box, and was met by a pile of instructions.

What do you do with the instructions? Like, when your wife orders a new shelf from the internet and it shows up with a booklet that's supposed to show you how to put it together. What do you do with that?

There are two kinds of people. There are people who follow the instructions. And, there are people who don't. Which one are you?

I'm an instructions kind of guy. Do you know why? Because I have tried putting it all together without the instructions. I've tried doing it with only half of the instructions. Because I'm not the one who designed the shelf it just goes better for me with the instructions.

So I got out the instructions and started putting my saw together. It took about five minutes. It probably should have taken half as long, but the instructions were terrible.

What do you do when you try to use the instructions and they suck? I've opened instructions only to discover they were written in a different language. I've been puzzled over instructions that didn't even use words. And I've scratched my head over Ikea instructions.

The instructions that came with my saw were way too complicated. Especially for a tool that was already mostly assembled. Seriously, it only needed two screws installed, but it came with a two hundred page instruction manual. There were some important pages, like the ones showing me how to keep from cutting off my fingers. And there were some useless pages–which was most of them.

What I've learned putting stuff together over the years is that there are two kinds of instructions—those that work, and those that don't. Some instructions stink. Some are near perfect. Some instructions are so complicated the entire process takes hours. Some are so simple I have to think through why they were even necessary.

The complicated instructions fail me when I get lost in the details. I forget why part A and part J need to intersect with part W while I'm trying to hold them all in my hand and look at the picture again. It can be an exercise in frustration. The simple instructions make it easy. Almost like magic the process is intuitive and the project just seems to fly together almost on its own.

I get why some things would need complicated instructions. I hope the guys who put my car together followed all of the complicated instructions. I hoped the same thing for the guys who performed my dad's heart surgery.

What I don't get is why simple things sometimes

come with complicated instructions. I don't know why something with two steps needs fifty pages. Just tell me the steps already.

Unfortunately I've met many people who show up in pursuit of Jesus but are met by overly complicated steps. This happens when someone decides to see if everyday with Jesus is better than any day without him, but they are handed a ridiculous set of instructions.

The Bible can seem super complicated. But what it all boils down to is what Jesus told his friends. Love God with all of your heart, soul, mind, and strength. Prove it by loving your neighbor. That's where it gets real. Don't wait for complicated instructions, just go where Jesus is pointing–across the street. If you want to love your neighbor, you've got to love the people in your path.

PROVE IT

One Sunday I stood in front of the hundreds of people at my church and told them some of the same stories I just shared with you. I talked about the importance of applying what we've learned, I talked about looking at the words of Jesus as something we are supposed to do, not just something we're supposed to know.

When I got home later that afternoon I had a message from my neighbor. She needed help fixing a doggy door. It was like Jesus peaked his holy head into the middle of my agenda and said, "you talk a big game, now prove it." There went my plans for a nap in the hammock.

I know they get tired of it sometimes, but I'm always looking for a chance to teach my kids what God is teaching me. So, I rounded up my boys and headed across the street. When we got to the neighbor's house I immediately saw the problem with the doggy door. But there was another problem. I don't know anything about little doggy doors because our dog uses normal doors.

I explained to my neighbor that I didn't really know anything about how to fix her situation and she explained to me like Princess Leia from Star Wars we were her only hope. I knew the situation was pretty dire if she was betting on my mediocre handyman skills so we gave it our best shot.

She didn't have a new door so we had to make do by fixing the old one the best we could. There weren't any instructions so I had to wing it. Thankfully my dad had given me lots of chances to fix things growing up. All I had to do was apply what my Father had taught me.

The other wrinkle was that the surroundings were a little gross. The broken door exited into a huge cage in my neighbor's backyard. By huge cage I mean bathroom. Because the door was busted her dog couldn't get outside to do its business. No wonder she was desperate.

It wasn't lost on me the awesome irony of the moment. Like Jesus was reminding me that sometimes when we do what he says or go where he goes we'll still wind up in a crappy situation. It's pretty much guaranteed. Because Jesus moved toward people who needed him, and people are messy.

If we're going to be people who make a habit out of doing what Jesus said, we'll never run out of chances to prove we were listening. You'll know another chance is coming your way when you look out your window over breakfast and see the sun peaking over the horizon. Everyday with Jesus is a chance to choose if we will do what he said. I don't always get it right, but that day I did. I loved my neighbor and her nasty little dog.

CHAPTER 22
PRAY LIKE JESUS

STRUGGLE

Praying can be a real head-scratcher. I mean, a lot of us, myself included, have had our struggles with prayer. I've got a laundry list of reasons why I used to wrestle with it. But you know what? I wanted to get to the bottom of this, so I went out and asked around, and I was reminded I wasn't alone.

Some folks said it's like they're playing a guessing game with God. Others, they're so self-conscious, it's like they're on stage at a talent show being judged by the whole universe. Finding the right words? Man, that's a real puzzle. And don't get me started on feeling overwhelmed or finding the time–life's already got more items on the to-do list than there are grains of sand at the beach!

Let me take you back to a time when I was as clueless as a cat at a dog show. My students and I decided to sign up for an all-night prayer vigil during an election. We took the graveyard shift from midnight to 5 AM. While my students were praying their hearts out, I headed into my office and took a nap. Terrible, I know, but at that point, I had no idea how to pray!

You know what I've learned? Praying is only hard if you're doing it wrong. I spent most of my life thinking prayer was like trying to juggle torches while riding a unicycle on a tightrope–impossible. And then I saw someone do it.

Maybe your prayer life has felt that way , too.too. Do you know the one prayer God never, and I mean never, answers? It's the one you don't pray!

Thank the heavens for all those praying moms and grandmas out there. They had the foresight to pray for what we needed, even when we didn't know it ourselves. It might just be the reason you're reading this book.

WHAT'S THE DEAL

Why don't we pray? What's the deal with that? Do we want God's favor to breeze past us? Heck no. Do we want our sins to pile up like laundry? Absolutely not. Do we want to miss out on blessing or divine help? Of course not. So why don't we pray?

Some of you reading this are probably praying machines. You're what we often call prayer warriors. When that movie *War Room* hit the screens, you grabbed your Bible and journal and went to the movies like it was a pilgrimage. You enjoy praying, and you're darn good at it. Thank you! Please keep it up.

But then there's folks like me. We start to pray, and it's like trying to catch a firefly with a spoon—all over the place. We get distracted, uncomfortable, or we're stumped for words. Our words seem like scattered pebbles when spoken to the Rock of Ages.

We just don't know how to pray. So, what do we do? We don't pray at all. And that's a tragedy, because we should be able to talk to God about anything. He wants to hear from us. God loves hearing from us.

LIKE JESUS

One day Jesus was praying, and His disciples heard Him. Now, do you think they'd never heard a prayer before? Come on, they weren't living under a rock. What was so compelling about Jesus' prayer that made them want to learn? They straight-up said, "Master, teach us!"

When Jesus prayed, things happened. Dead folks strolled out of tombs, blind eyes started functioning, wobbly limbs found strength, even demons couldn't help but shiver. Heaven itself perked up when Jesus prayed. So, why wouldn't we want to pray like Jesus?

When we pray like Jesus things will change. And for some of us, that's exactly what we need. It's not about controlling God; that would be absurd. It is about having access to Him. When you're living every day with Jesus you have access to God himself. It changes everything.

Now, what if I told you that you could learn to pray like Jesus? Here's the catch, learning alone won't cut it. Learning without applying it? That's like owning a bike but never hitting the trails. But we can learn to pray confidently about anything, just like Jesus. So, here's the first prayer we all need to pray: "Jesus, teach me to pray."

How did Jesus pray? Well, you've probably heard of the Lord's Prayer. It's the second-most famous prayer, right after the "God is good, God is great" dinner anthem.

But guess what? It's our blueprint for prayer. This is what teaches us to pray like Jesus.

THE LORD'S PRAYER

Picture the Lord's Prayer as Jesus' instructions for how to connect with God. It's not a magic recipe for your words. It's not a cosmic formula we need to get just right. It's a guide that connects our sometimes confused hearts to a really loving Father. This isn't a blueprint about complex architectural jargon; it's a straightforward path to a strong foundation with God.

It's really one prayer that Jesus prayed to teach his friends, but what makes it so beautiful is that it's also several prayers. Think of it like a scaffolding for connecting with God. It's gratitude, forgiveness, and hope all propping up the faith we desire. Each of these prayers are incredibly versatile. You can pray each of them individually or string them together. This is how Jesus prayed.

Jesus prayed "our Father in heaven, hallowed be your name," This statement is a moment of acknowledgement. God is not some distant deity; He's our Heavenly Dad. He loves us more than we can imagine. It's a moment of recognizing how amazing and holy God is. It's like saying, "Wow, God, you're incredible, and I want everyone to know it!"

Another way of praying this is to say, "God, reveal yourself." This prayer is a powerful anchor for us. In the midst of life's craziness, when you find yourself scratching your head, wondering what's going on, this is the prayer you turn to. "God reveal yourself!" It's a reminder that even when we can't comprehend what's happening, a Holy God is right by our side. I prayed this when my brother faced cancer, by my grandma's deathbed, and when life unraveled during my senior year of college.

Jesus' next part of the familiar prayer was "your kingdom come, your will be done, on earth as it is in heaven." It's like saying, "God, let your dreams for the world come true, just like they do in heaven. Help us live like you want us to." In it we are acknowledging that not everything around us is as it ought to be. We're asking God to make the world a better place. We're asking God to make it right.

When life goes off the rails, when something's messed up, this is the prayer you need. Whether you've been wronged or faced an injustice, you boldly proclaim your trust in God, saying, "God, make it right." It's like saying, "I trust You more than I trust myself." Remember, we often leave that part off, but if we truly want what's right, we need to ask God to make it right.

Jesus also said, "give us today our daily bread". This one's all about asking God to provide what we need for today. It's like saying, "Hey God, could you help me out with today's to-do list?" Another way of saying this would be, "God, provide for me." This one may feel more familiar because it's where we often treat prayer like a wish list. It's crucial to express your needs clearly to God, just as Jesus taught his friends. In this we learn to strike a balance between what we want and what we truly need. Tell God your desires, but trust Him for your necessities.

Forgiveness is a big deal to Jesus. He didn't leave that out of his instructional prayer when he said, "and forgive us our debts, as we also have forgiven our debtors." It's like a giant eraser for our mistakes. We're saying, "God, please forgive us for the mess-ups, just like we're learning to forgive others.

This prayer is a lifeline. When you've stumbled, made mistakes, or messed up, don't hesitate to say, "God, forgive me." This is a pivotal prayer, one you can approach with unwavering confidence because Jesus paid the price for you to do so. If you need to utter this prayer today, don't hold back.

The second part of the forgiveness prayer is no less

important. Jesus made it clear that holding onto unforgiveness can come between you and God. So, if you need to forgive someone, have an honest conversation with God about it. Say, "God, help me forgive," and He will. Whether it's your neighbor, friend, spouse, or even yourself, don't let unforgiveness hijack your relationship with God.

Jesus also wanted us to know we didn't have to wait until after we've messed up to ask for help. He taught us friends this, "do not bring us into temptation." This part is like asking God to help us steer clear of trouble and keep us safe from anything that could hurt us. This prayer is your go-to when you find yourself repeatedly getting in your own way. If you could use some help avoiding your own pitfalls, this is the prayer for you. Don't be embarrassed to ask for assistance.

Remember, you won't always be your own worst enemy, and that's why Jesus gave us the final part of this prayer, "but deliver us from the evil one". You might have heard this term used in various contexts, usually regarding someone caught up in a troublesome situation. It's our way of asking God to break the spiritual chains that bind us. If you feel trapped, say, "God, deliver me." Whether you're caught in a mess or facing something that's holding you back, this prayer has the power to set you free.

JUST ONE WEEK

Prayer gives you access to God, and that's a game-changer. You don't need fancy words or theatrical performances. Just be real, just say it, like you're chatting with your closest friend. There's no need to stress about "getting it right" or striving for perfection. We're all going to stumble over our words along the way. That's perfectly normal. We're here to learn from Jesus not improvise a poetic masterpiece.

When you incorporate these prayers into your daily life, the way you pray will fundamentally change. For some of us that's precisely what we need. Prayer gives you access to God through faith because he is right there with you waiting for you to do your part. What does this mean for us? How does it affect our lives? It's a game-changer! It means we can pray confidently about anything. Prayer is not a negotiation; it's a conversation with your loving Father.

Jesus emphasized the importance of being direct with God. Don't try to bargain or beat around the bush. Just tell Him what you need. He loves hearing it from you, so say it boldly, plainly, and with confidence. Remember, there's no need to put on a show.

In *Learn Love Live* I told the story of visiting Jamie's grandma on her deathbed. I was so mad at God because I witnessed this saintly woman was suffering. I couldn't even find the words to comfort my wife. I went home, entered our spare bedroom, and just let God have it. It was an ugly prayer, not theatrical or fancy, just me and

God. It was precisely the opportunity He had been waiting for because I wasn't fixated on the outcome; I was focused on nurturing my inner relationship with God. It was real, genuine, and it changed my prayer life forever.

When you stop obsessing over the words you use or how you say them, and you get real about what's on your heart, everything changes. Many times, we're too caught up in trying to be better versions of ourselves instead of striving to be more like Jesus. If prayer has felt like a struggle, chances are you've been doing it wrong, but that can change – you can pray like Jesus.

Just one week of praying these prayers will transform how you view prayer. Take the challenge. Pray these prayers everyday for a week. Pray them at home. Pray them at work. Pray them when you're picking your kids from school. Pray them at the dentist and the dollar store. For one week pray everyday like Jesus. One week will change a lot, but if you make it a habit it will change your life.

CHAPTER 23
LOVE AND NOISE

NIRVANA

Rewind to August 1998: There I was, young and ready to take on the world. Only to realize college was like a puzzle where all the pieces come from a different box. I was suddenly seeing things Sunday school never prepared me for.

I was enthusiastic about it so I attempted to share my faith. Every time I sounded meaner than a cat in a bath. The reason? I was all about the rulebook, not the love story. I remember strolling around the university campus with Brad, serenading unsuspecting folks with our rendition of Nirvana's "Lake of Fire." Can you imagine the reactions when we belted out, "Where do bad folks go when they die? They don't go to heaven where the angels fly. They go to the lake of fire and fry..." Not exactly life giving stuff. We'd finish with the classic line, "... See them again on the fourth of July." I don't know what Independance Day has to do with heaven and hell, but the guy who wrote that song did a lot of drugs.

I know this won't surprise you, but my approach had the same success rate as throwing a marshmallow at a bank vault. We weren't getting in. It didn't take before I began to realize I was off-course. I decided to call a time-out on all the stuff the church I grew up in called "witnessing". In the meantime I hit the big fat reset button on a lot of what I believed. I decided to keep only my faith in Jesus and respect for the Bible. Deep down, I knew Jesus had my back. Over time, it became clear to me that people just needed Jesus. They didn't need my fancy words or a sidewalk circus act. My job wasn't to be anyone's spiritual referee. If anything I was supposed to be Jesus' hype man everywhere I went. Only, with a lot more hope and a lot less hype.

NOISE

During college I played a lot of rock and roll music. I traveled all over the place playing music with my friends. I'd shred on the guitar and scream songs into the microphone about life and Jesus. Meanwhile each of my friends would do their part. One guy would thump out loud booming notes on the bass. Another dude played power chords that laid out the melody. And our drummer would sit on stage with the shiniest cymbals you've ever seen. He'd raise his hands again and again crashing home in a cascading cacophony of sound.

Par for the course for rock music at the turn of the century we were pretty predictable in our songs. There was always a moment when the song would have a break. It would get quiet or change tones. The moment in the song was designed to build tension and get everyone to lean in. They'd anticipate the beautiful or at least awesome sound to come. Our songs would always build to a moment like that, but then... clang. The cymbals would erupt in noise. It was loud. Sometimes it even made people jump. But it usually lacked the harmony everyone expected. This is what it's like to communicate without love.

Paul the apostle warned some friends about speaking about their faith this way. He told them love was paramount when it came to sharing their faith. Every word has to originate in love. When it doesn't you're just making noise. Looking back on many of the times I tried to share my faith all I can remember is a lot of noise.

You might be the loudest voice in the room. You may have the vocabulary of Shakespeare and the eloquence of a seasoned orator. But without love, your words are just a performance. It's like trying to play a song without tuning your instrument; people may hear you, but will they listen?

You can't fake love. And you can't make your love

about making a point. It's not about winning an argument. It's not about putting on a show so people who agree with you like what you have to say. It's not about getting God to applaud your performance. It's about genuine, raw, unfiltered love. The kind of love that you can't contain, the kind that spills over into every word you say, every action you take.

Next time you're gearing up to make a point or win a debate, take a second. Tune your heart strings. Are you about to sound loving or are you just making noise? At the end of the day, love doesn't just make you heard, it makes you felt. Love is what changes hearts and minds. How you present it matters.

PRESENTATION MATTERS

I enthusiastically stepped into a chiropractor's clinic for the very first time after watching a few youtube videos about back pain. Because, surprise, my back hurt. Hey, I'm all about those new experiences.

Now, imagine my surprise when my chiropractor turned out to be this ancient dude with the social skills of a boiled potato. He had an eerie ability to avoid eye contact at the precise wrong moments. There I was, folded into some sort of human origami, when the old man leaned over on top of me whispering, "It's ok. I got you." Creepy.

He was a tiny guy. I don't know what I was expecting. But then he did some kind of Jiu Jitsu move. If I'd known chiropractors were part-time professional wrestlers, I might have reconsidered. He kept saying, "It's ok. I got you." But let's be honest, at that moment, what he 'got' was a grown man trying not to freak out. Then–SNAP! My neck made a sound reminiscent of a popcorn machine at full throttle. I half-expected a marching band to kick open the door, given how much my spine resembled their halftime drum solo.

Here's the twist (pun intended): I walked into that clinic, expecting some minor back adjustment. But the creepy doctor revealed the core issue – my wonky hips. I was strolling around, blissfully unaware, thinking I was in ship-shape. It's funny, isn't it? How can we miss something so fundamental about ourselves? It's akin to seeking answers for a slight itch and discovering you're actually part werewolf.

After I wobbled out of his creepy lair, I couldn't help but think that the whole thing could have been so much smoother if he'd just invested in some conversational skills. You know, the kind you'd expect from someone who gets up close and personal with your vertebrae?

His grasp of the technique was solid. But in terms of presentation? Let's just say it hovered somewhere between an awkward distant relative and belt sander on a chalkboard. I wasn't expecting stand-up comedy, but a smile goes a long way. Not coming off like the creepy Spine Whisperer helps, too. Knowing one's craft and being able to present it in a way that doesn't feel like an audition for a low-budget horror film? Two totally different skill sets.

Sometimes we do the same thing with our faith.

We're handed this breathtakingly beautiful message of love, redemption, and grace. Like we've been entrusted with the world's most precious diamond. But then, instead of showcasing it in a way that truly magnifies its beauty, we stuff it into a sock. Why? Because we're just going through the motions. Perhaps we think that's what we're supposed to do. Instead of sharing out of overflowing joy and love, we're sharing out of routine. It's like having the most delicious cake ever but serving it on a garbage can lid. The flavor doesn't change, but presentation affects the appetite.

NO POP QUIZ

Would you rather have a conversation with someone about the love of God, or sucker someone into a game of Bible trivia? Personally, I'd sooner take another trip to my creepy old chiropractor than wind up in another conversation about obscure Old Testament facts.

It's a bit tricky, because sometimes in our zeal we act like overenthusiastic salespeople. Imagine walking into a store for some socks and being barraged with a monologue about wool extraction in the Andes. Interesting? Maybe. Relevant? Not so much.

Jesus made what he hopes we'll do pretty clear. He wants us to share his good news. The news that he loves everyone and hopes they'll come to him to find out first hand.

Somewhere along the way, many of us started

thinking this meant giving elaborate theological dissertations, or to opine our take on some social issue. Instead of introducing folks to the heart of Jesus, we've sometimes bamboozled them with so much jargon and trivia they're left feeling like they've been contorted.

Instead of ambushing them with a pop quiz about how many people Jesus fed, what if we actually fed their hearts? People are hungry for authenticity and love, not religious riddles.

Here's the simple truth: Everyday with Jesus is better than any day without Him. I mean, take it from someone who's sat through countless theological debates and, yes, that one unforgettable chiropractor visit. More often than not, we forget that the heart of our message isn't in the complexity but in the beautiful simplicity of Jesus' love.

The core of our faith is a relationship built on love, not a task list built on duty. It's not about checking boxes or meeting quotas. It's about sharing an encounter, a story, an experience with Jesus. When you genuinely love something, you can't help but share it, not out of obligation, but out of overflowing joy. And the beautiful thing is, when we approach sharing our faith like this, it's infectious. People won't just hear our words; they'll feel the warmth of our passion and the genuine love behind every syllable.

Our calling isn't to dazzle with elaborate religious discourse or to get lost in the theological woods. Instead, it's to showcase through our lives how spending everyday with Jesus beats any day without Him. We aim to make every interaction count.

When sharing our faith becomes something we feel we have to do, rather than something we get to do we're in trouble. When we switch from an "I have to" to an "I get to" mentality, everything changes. We stop running through rehearsed lines and elevator pitches. We stop making noise. We begin sharing the most important piece of our hearts. The story of Jesus isn't a sales pitch; it's a love letter written across your heart. We don't share it because it's a duty, but because it's a delight.

We're all living examples of the crazy love and grace Jesus has for us. My kids don't prance around reciting our house rules to every stranger at the park. But for those paying attention their words and actions are an important commentary about the way they are loved.

The same goes for our faith. Sharing Jesus isn't about delivering a rehearsed argument. It's about sharing your unique story, plot twists, hangups, and failures included. We don't sugar coat it. We just invite someone in. Be the genuine, quirky, salt-of-the-earth person you are. Discuss the times you tripped over your own feet, the days you felt on top of the world, and the moments when you weren't sure which way was up.

When you open up about both your hang ups and your high points, it strikes a chord. One that sounds a lot less like noise. People can relate to the not-so-perfect, because we've all been there.

COMMON GROUND

A couple of years back, I found myself with an invitation to the Secular Human Alliance at the local university. Of course I went. I love invitations. But I had no idea what I was wandering into. I half-expected it to be a room full of board game enthusiasts or perhaps a support group for people who put pineapple on pizza. To my surprise, it was a whole tribe of folks who weren't the biggest fans of Christians. They didn't seem to have a problem with Jesus, but they had a laundry list of issues with those of us claiming to spend everyday with him. And they weren't shy about it.

I have run into this collective eyebrow raise towards our faith quite a bit over the years. But I didn't go there to preach. I didn't pack in my best Sunday school answers. I didn't even sing any Nirvana. In fact, no one in the meeting except for the club president knew I was a pastor. I didn't show up to be heard. I went to make friends. Before the conversation turned tense we played some games, had some snacks, and did what new friends do. It was pretty normal people stuff. We weren't people on different sides of an agenda. We were people gathered around a plate of cookies.

As the conversation turned toward the business at hand I realized that their disdain for Christianity wasn't really about the grand questions of the universe. While they offered up suggestions for hosting an on campus debate between science and faith it became obvious that their gripe was more... personal. It was about their past run-ins with folks who claimed to be spending everyday with Jesus but maybe played fast and loose with loving their neighbor. They weren't people who were mad at Jesus, they were just allergic to all the noise the Christians they had bumped into kept making. They couldn't stand the holier than thou attitudes, the judgmental glances, and the never ending condescension couched in political and social posturing.

Sitting in that room that night I realized something critical. Most of the people around us don't get the church drill. They don't know why we assemble in big buildings to belt out what looks like our own subcultural karaoke. They don't understand why we get teary-eyed over age-old stories. They're bewildered by our stances on things. To many, our faith seems alien or, worse, insincere.

If we want a real connection, if we want to share this amazing love we've found, we need common ground. So, step one: learn to engage people where they are in their own lives. Drop the script and fully engage who they are. Next, give them the benefit of the doubt. Try seeing the world through their eyes for five minutes. You don't have to do what they do or believe what they believe in order to see they are loved. You don't have to agree with them. But you do have to stop trying to make them agree with you for five minutes. The most important part of sharing what Jesus is doing in your life everyday is to embrace those who haven't figured it out yet with an open heart. When we turn down the noise in favor of genuine love we will find common ground.

DO YOU WANT TO

About a decade ago I helped start up a new gathering for students at a church. One night, after one of our services, a young man named Nathan strolled up to me. I could see in his eyes that he was searching.

"I'm not sure I believe in God anymore," he declared. He launched into a line of questioning like a shopping list of all the biggest arguments against faith. It was like being handed a pop quiz for a class I hadn't attended in years. We talked about science. We brushed up against philosophy. We delved into what he deemed ridiculous. Week after week he kept coming back for more.

He wasn't there for music. To him it was just noise. He didn't show up to make friends. Nope. Nathan came to vent. He wanted to unload about everything he hated about Christians. Truthfully, he'd seen a side of it that would make anyone cringe. So, I listened. For weeks I listened.

One evening, after I'd answered what felt like his thousandth question, I sensed a change. It was as if he had thrown every curveball he had and was all out of ammunition. "Nathan," I gently started, "How about I share my story with you?"

I shared some stories about my childhood. I talked

about growing up in church on Sundays and the loving family I was fortunate to have. All of this was foreign to his experience. Then I shifted to familiar terrain–the good, the bad, and the ugly of Christian behavior. Every gripe he had, I acknowledged through the lens of my journey.

Pausing, I looked straight into his eyes, "Nathan, it feels like our perspectives aren't all that different." He nodded, noncommittal. Venturing further, I said, "It sounds like you've been burnt by some not-so-loving people?"

With a quiver in his voice, he admitted, "That's spot on."

Taking a deep breath, I ventured, "The game-changer for me was realizing how much God loved me. It doesn't seem like you've ever experienced that."

His next statement was a big acknowledgment, "I think you're right."

So I asked the question we all have to eventually ask if we're sincere about sharing Jesus with others, "Do you want to experience the real love of Jesus?"

His eyes welled up, emotion spilling over, "I really do," was all he could muster.

There in the middle of the hallway, surrounded by the noise of people picking up their kids, Nathan truly understood God's love for him for the first time. I prayed with him as we both shed happy tears.

It wasn't about winning a debate or acing all his questions. Nathan felt God's pull, not because of water-tight arguments, but because I listened. I heard his heart. I shared my own. We got all the noise out of the way and let Jesus lead us both toward common ground. The kind of common ground Jesus always points to when we stop making noise and start walking everyday in love.

CHAPTER 24
GOOD FRUIT

OBVIOUS

Every summer for as long as I can remember has been watermelon season on my family's farm. My Dad has grown them for decades. I have spent thousands of hours working with watermelons in the hot summer sun.

After months of work it was always exciting to harvest the first watermelon of the season. Dad would reach down and feel the bright green surface. If it was rough and bumpy rather than smooth that was a good sign the fruit was ripe. Then he'd start to roll it over and check it's belly. If the belly was dull instead of bright that was another good sign. Sometimes as he'd begin to roll one over something gross would happen. It would just kind of collapse in on itself in a squishy mess. Why? Because the belly was soft and the fruit was bad.

Have you ever bitten into bad fruit? If so, the shock

and surprise of it is not something you soon forget. You're expecting something sweet and instead you get something nasty. Bad fruit is soft and squishy. It often stinks. It attracts bugs and other undesirable things. Bad fruit doesn't add value to your life.

If we look around our world right now it's hard not to see the result of a lot of bad fruit. People seem angrier than ever. Opinions and feelings seem to be driving the narrative on the regular. Mental and emotional struggles have hit an all time high. There just seems to be so many problems. But all of this is less than what God wants us to experience as his kids. We could stay messed up about it and let it ruin the moment. Or we can remember God always has a solution for bad things.

In the time of Jesus the Jews were living with the fruit of hundreds of years of bad decisions. Life was hard. Their nation had been occupied. Their religion was corrupted by greedy men. And, to many, God seemed silenced.

Then John the Baptizer showed up. He was there to prepare the way for Jesus. Because God always has a solution for bad things. John wasn't the solution. He was there to soften them up for the real solution, Jesus. He did it by preaching one singular message, "produce the right kind of fruit in the way you live. Fruit that shows everyone you've repented."

If we lean into the words of John we'll lean away from the bad fruit in our lives. Our life like our heart will turn toward God. It's what God wanted for the folks John spoke to on the banks of the Jordan River. And it's what he wants for you and I. But how do we actually do it? How do we produce fruit in keeping with repentance?

Choose to live in a way that adds value to your life and the lives around you. Choose good fruit. You get to choose. You get to decide what is in your home. You get to decide what is in your life. You get to choose what is in your heart. Producing fruit in keeping with repentance is a moment-to-moment exercise in loving your neighbor and loving God.

Your fruit should be obvious. When you look at an apple tree during harvest there's no doubt what kind of tree it is. A heart producing the fruit of repentance won't be confused for something else.

Your fruit should keep growing. You'll know it's growing when you have more than you need. The overflow of what God is doing in your own heart becomes a source of joy for the folks around you.

The litmus test John the Baptizer offered up were actions that moved his listeners toward peace, kindness, goodness, and self-control. These are some of the things that are obvious, shared, and growing in the lives of anyone living a life of repentance. Paul added love, joy, forbearance, faithfulness, and gentleness to John's list.

The thing about fruit is that it only comes from something full of life. John wanted his contemporaries to experience the fullness of life with God. He was preparing their hearts for the work Jesus would do. Jesus's sacrificial act of amazing love showed us the way to God. The one John had been preparing the people for.

So the big question you and I have to deal with is this; Are these things evident in my life? If the answer was yes our heart is turned toward God. We have a heart continually prepared for the Lord to do something amazing. We are steeped in joy and overflowing in graciousness. That's a good life and it brings us an inward peace and steadiness that blesses those around us.

When John the Baptizer told the religious guys in the bible to "bear fruit in keeping with repentance" he wasn't talking about growing strawberries. He wasn't referring to the kind of fruit you grow on a vine or the kind you pluck from a tree. John was talking about what gets cultivated in your heart.

Good fruit doesn't show up in our lives because we want applause. But it does show up when we are growing into people who spend everyday with Jesus. It grows because that's what living things do. As you spend your days learning to live more and more like Jesus the fruit becomes obvious. It's like looking for an orange surrounded by broccoli–it won't be hard to find. If the people around you can't find it–it's not obvious. And, if it's not obvious, it's not there. Keep growing. Today is the perfect day to turn it around. To ask God to help you produce fruit in your life. Fruit that helps rather than hurts. Fruit that leads to repentance. Fruit that will ultimately bring you back to him. What are you waiting for?

IN AND OUT

My tone often reflects what I'm letting in. For instance, if I've watched too much reality TV, I'm probably more likely to use the word "dramatic" in casual conversation. Funny how that works, right? Things like anger, selfishness, and unforgiveness? That stuff likes to sneak in like ants in the spring. You know they are there somewhere, but they show up when you least expect it.

Speaking of surprises, we kept hearing this bizarre sound downstairs when we were trying to sleep. Jamie nudged me one night, eyes wide, whispering, "Did you hear that in the garage?!". Either we had a burglar with a peculiar sense of humor, or my tools all decided to start jumping off their shelves. Armed with my pistol and a serious case of bed hair, I went to the garage and found–absolutely nothing. The next morning I found the culprit. A squirrel had gotten on the top shelf and spilled cans of paint everywhere.

We have to be careful what we let in. We don't want anything sneaking into our lives–especially the squirrely stuff. Over the last couple of years, there's been an uptick in negative emotions and actions–just flip through the channels and see. You don't have to go far to see bad fruit everywhere! If you've ever bitten into a rotten apple, you know that not all surprises are pleasant. Because life seems so full of bad fruit, let's be people who aim to bear good fruit.

The Apostle Paul wrote a bunch of letters that are included in the bible, but before he started living everyday with Jesus he was part of the gang of religious guys John the Baptizer was always agitating. These guys may have looked like they had it all together, but their fruit was questionable. Later Paul would call out people like this. Probably because he was glad Jesus had shown him a better way to live. When he wrote his letter to some friends in Galatia he was passionate about it, not because he was mad at them–he just wanted them to know how to live out the freedom of genuine faith. He told them a laundry list of bad things to stay away from. Not because he was trying to ruin their fun, but because he knew how much better everyday with Jesus was.

THE LIST

When you live with Jesus everyday, good stuff grows. Paul wrote us a list. It's like a grocery list for all of the best things you can have in your life. I'm talking about love, joy, peace, and all those things we wish came in a cereal box every morning. These are the kinds of fruit life with Jesus displayed.

When it comes to the good fruit God longs for us to experience, love wins the blue ribbon. When you give away the last piece of the pie–that's love. If you've ever smiled at a barista who messed up your order–that's love. Those may seem like small things, but they're big things when they are the fruit of love.

Love in action was always meant to be the calling card of people spending everyday following Jesus.

Because everywhere Jesus went and everything Jesus did was about the next person he was always on his way to love. We've all been the recipient of love like that. The invitation to follow Jesus everyday means being given the greenlight to participate in love on a scale beyond imagination. When you do you won't be able to keep yourself from giving it away. The best part is that life gets a little sweeter for everyone who accepts the invitation.

Joy shows up, too. It shows up again and again. I'm not talking about mere happiness. Joy isn't what you feel when you find $20 in an old pair of jeans. Joy is deeper, longer-lasting, and doesn't vanish when you get cut off in traffic.

Joy is like an invisible glow coming from the inside. You sense joy in the countenance of someone who refuses to be bossed around by hard times. When someone is full of joy they don't let a bad day tell them how they're supposed to treat the people around them. People who have filled up on joy don't have room for the negative by-products of their circumstances.

When I'm sitting at the terminal in a busy airport I really love my noise-canceling headphones. It feels like peace, but it's a distant second. Peace is the quiet confidence that everything is going to be alright. Peace blossoms when we follow Jesus. Human nature might feel like an old GPS shouting "recalculating" for the seventeenth time. Peace is a certainty that surpasses our human understanding. Peace blossoms in the spaces where we make room to trust Jesus.

If patience had a knob you could crank up to eleven it would be forbearance. It sounds like a fancy word your grandma used. Forbearance isn't waiting for your phone to charge because you let the battery drop to 3%. It is what happens when you live with both tolerance and restraint.

The world around us has lost the plot where tolerance is concerned. True tolerance is when you're not in agreement, but you are in peace. When I was a kid a group calling themselves the "moral majority" seemed to have all the power. Because they were the loudest voice of the day it seemed like they got to decide what tolerance looked like. These days there are a lot of loud voices vying for their shot at the wheel. What no one seems to be practicing is the restraint essential to forbearance.

When Jesus is helping us grow forbearance in our lives we ask this question before we act, "will doing this demonstrate love?" If the answer is "no", then the action is not producing good fruit in our lives.

Live with the tolerance of restraint. That's forbearance. Don't be the snarky one with a snide comment. Don't be a keyboard warrior. Jesus isn't looking for people eager to enforce rules, but he delights in God's sons and daughters who are willing to walk with him daily.

Kindness is what grows when we live with the good old-fashioned "golden rule". Your elementary school teacher didn't make that up, Jesus did. Not only did he actually live it, but he is inviting you and I to step into a life full of kindness, too. Did you know kindness is what caused Christianity to grow like a wildfire. What if your kindness was the first spark to what happens next?

Goodness is what it's like when your moral compass doesn't need Google Maps. It's doing the right thing even when no one is watching. Goodness is a bit ironic because those who obsess over living a moral life are often the least loving. Jesus never meant for it to be that way.

Goodness is not the point of spending everyday with Jesus. But goodness is one result of spending everyday with Jesus. When morality becomes the focus of your life with God–you better look up, because you stopped following Jesus. A life built around pursuing morality is just virtue signaling. It's not a life focused on spending everyday with Jesus. Don't become a slave to morality. Become someone really good at loving what Jesus loves.

Out of everything on Paul's list to his friends, faithfulness is probably my favorite. Every year my friend Mark asks me, "Nate, what are you dreaming about this year." My answer hasn't changed in a decade. I always tell him I want to be faithful. I want to be faithful to my church. I want to be faithful to the beautiful brunette bombshell I'm married to. I want to be faithful to my kids. And, I want to be faithful to the everyday opportunities God puts in front of me.

Faithfulness is what happens when God hands you

a possibility and you say "yes". Do it once and it's an opportunity. Do it everyday and it's faithfulness.

Do you want to know how faithful you really are? Give someone who loves you permission to help you list your habits. How you're handling your everyday opportunities is summed up by your habits. Are you being faithful to what you're being trusted with? If not, turn it around. If you are. Awesome. Keep being faithful.

About an hour after my son Jon was first born, my parents brought my oldest son Ethan into the room. His first words to his baby brother were so sweet, "Ok, baby we go play." I know. Sweet, right?

Genteless is sweet. With a baby you always have to tell the older kids the same thing over and over, "Gentle. Gentle. Gentle." Look, gentleness is what helps us remember not everyone is at the same place in their journey. Gentleness is about moving through life with care. Helping to look out for the one who can't walk on their own yet.

Jesus always walked toward the people who needed him with gentleness. If you want to know if you are living with gentleness ask yourself this question, "Do I move toward the people who need Jesus?" If the answer is no, it's time to turn it around.

You are a complicated mixture of psychology, brain chemistry, physical impulses, emotional responses, and spiritual inclinations. That's a fancy way of saying there are a lot of things pulling your strings. But even so, you don't have to be a puppet to your impulses. That's precisely what Paul was trying to get his friends to understand with all his talk about fruit.

You were set free to live a free life. Living everyday with Jesus means you're free. You can live with self-control. You get to vote for the kind of life you want to live.

Do you know what happens when your life starts looking like the list of fruit Paul wrote about? It gets pretty sweet. Fruit is cool like that. The world around us could do with more people of faith pumping out heaps of the fruit on Paul's list. We can't afford to live any other way. Not if we care about letting those around us experience the fruit of every day with Jesus.

CHAPTER 25
PROOF

THE HARD QUESTION

One year after my breakfast with Roger the Soldier I got a text message out of the blue from my friend Wes. Wes was a student in the college group I helped lead for years. We were pretty tight. We'd go rock climbing together, meet up for meals, basketball, and guy talk with a bunch of other fellas. He was always a fun guy. Everyone loved Wes.

Seeing Wes mature was a joy. He finished his engineering degree while showing everyone around him what following Jesus daily really looks like. He fell in love, got married, and in a short span, was blessed with three beautiful children. It was the kind of storybook happiness you'd raise a toast to.

The morning I met up for breakfast with Wes we sat in the exact same booth I had sat in with Roger a year earlier. Like Roger, Wes was in turmoil. Wes's turmoil wasn't a result of his bad habits or reckless life. And it hadn't happened because someone important had stepped out of his life. Wes's troubles were personal, yet different. Wes was struggling because of his deep love for people hit by a series of incredible difficulties. That morning over bacon and eggs he asked me the king of all questions. Wes asked, "How can I truly know God exists?"

Wes asked the question for a variety of reasons. One reason he asked was because his brilliant mind loved the challenge of understanding complex things. He was the kind of guy who built complicated machines for fun. Another reason for asking was that he was trying to find answers for his desperate loved ones. He hated seeing them in pain. Many people of faith arrive at Wes's question when navigating pain. "How can I know?"

Wow. Proof for the existence of God. That's a doozy. At least once a week someone will reach out online with some version of "Nate, how do you really know God exists?!"

THE WRONG ANSWERS

There are some incredible books out there that tackle all of the philosophical and scientific attempts to prove God's existence. I've read and love many of them. Before Jesus showed me a different way to navigate important conversations of faith I used to sit in rooms like the Secular Human Alliance and argue about proof for the existence of God. Back then I wasn't the kind of guy who would have taken weeks to listen to Nathan the atheist in the hallway after church. I wasn't the guy who would have been able to weather Wes's sincerity without a deep concern. I would have felt an overwhelming urge to unleash my barrage of prepared answers. Guys like me who have walked with Jesus for a while usually come armed with a lot of them.

Wes and I could have talked about the fine-tuning of the universe. We could have spent the morning addressing the overwhelming number of physicists who believe in God. One of my favorite discussions used to be talking about the fact that you can see. The engineering of your eyeball is incredible. Even though Wes was an engineer, that's not what we discussed that morning.

Wes and I didn't talk over the historical evidence for Jesus. We didn't examine the huge amount of archeological data that supports the Bible. We didn't argue over the millions of Jews that have prayed the prayer Jesus pointed out to the religious guys who grilled him, "Hear O Israel, the Lord our God…". And we didn't debate the fact that those same people we believe chosen by God have been targeted for genocide in every generation for the last 4,000 years.

A lot of that stuff could be used to aim at the existence of God. People a lot smarter than me have been doing it for years. But all of those things were outside of Wes's experience. All of those things are outside of your experience. Mine, too. They are all great answers.

They're all interesting conversations I used to love to have. They gave me a chance to be proud of how smart I am. But they were all the wrong answers for Wes.

That morning I sat across the table from my friend. A friend who already knew everyday with Jesus was better than any day without him. A guy I loved who had been living it just as surely as I was. At that moment, as I heard and saw Wes's pain I didn't want the canned answers for either of us. I wanted what Jesus has been teaching me over the last three decades. I wanted to remember how walking with Jesus everyday through the thick and the thin, the easy and the hard, the joy and the pain, all boils down to one simple truth. It takes faith to trust. Academic and philosophical jiu jitsu might be fun, but it's not loving. Real love is built on trust. And fundamentally trust takes faith.

EVIDENCE

Several years ago a young man told me "I don't believe in God and faith. I believe in science."

To which I replied, "I believe in science too, but did you do the experiments?"

"Well, no." He said.

"But you believe the experiments?" I questioned.

"Yes, of course." was his quick reply.

As soon as I said it, I could tell my final response was not what he expected, "and what do you think belief is?"

I asked my friend Wes the same thing over breakfast that day, "what do you think belief is?"

Everything takes faith. Anything worth believing in. I have faith that I will wake up tomorrow. Faith the grocery store will have food when I get there. Faith my car starts when I turn the key. Faith the sun will rise every morning. Anything we hope or believe takes faith. Here's the kicker. That's not proof for the existence of God either. Okay, what is the proof?

What if what you do and the way you show up in the lives of those around you is the biggest and best proof of God someone will ever see? A guy named Daniel in the Bible was a guy like that. You might remember Daniel from a story about a sleepover with lions after one too many prayers. That's an amazing story, but I'm talking about a different moment in Daniel's life.

Daniel and some of his friends had been taken as prisoners by an evil king and forced to serve him. When the king had a confusing dream he used his authority to command all of the smart guys in the kingdom to tell him what the dream meant. No one could do it so the king commanded all the people pretending to be wizards and soothsayers to interpret his dream. Still, no one could do it.

The king was furious so he issued an order that all the "wise men" be killed. Talk about overkill. In a cruel act of fate Daniel and his pals were lumped into the same category as all the phonies who'd failed the king. But Daniel wasn't to be deterred. He did what anyone who trusts God in faith would do–Daniel prayed about it. And God helped him.

In an act of characteristic boldness Daniel approached the king and asked him not to kill everyone. He promised the king would receive an answer about his confusing dream. The catch, Daniel said, was that men couldn't do what the king asked, but God would do it. And then God did. God showed Daniel the answer, Daniel told the king, and it blew his mind.

The king's response was a good one. Because of Daniel's humble faith he saw the reality of God. He didn't see it because of philosophy. He didn't land on the truth over prepared answers. The king saw a man willing to trust God with his life. The king saw a man who knew God and loved the people around him.

It wasn't the witty reply and the mental gymnastics that impressed the old cranky king. It was the combination of truth and love that did it. The truth intersected what the king had been seeking. Daniel was able to do it because of the way he was willing to love. Daniel's love in action was the evidence God is real.

PROOF

Wes and I spent most of our conversation that morning talking about God's love for us. We both got really honest about the ways life had thrown some tough stuff in our direction over the years. Things geared up to challenge every notion of love we'd come to rely on.

As our talk progressed I saw in my friend someone

with a hard question. The kind that a lot of people who walk with Jesus want to write off, ignore, or bulldoze with their big brained answers. I saw a husband, a father, a son, a brother, and a friend. Someone willing to waid into difficult water in order to find a truth he could carry home to the most important people in his life. The longer we talked the more clear the answer became.

Love is the bell ringer. It is the grand champion of evidence. It's the thing that rises above all the noise clamoring in our lives. Love is what will prove the existence of God to the people around you.

Not the broken cheap love as defined by the world around us. If we look at the way love is typically presented in our world it's pretty messed up. What our society calls love is often nothing more than some kind of mutually beneficial infatuation. It's about an attraction two people have for one another leading to some kind of benefit. That's not love. That's selfishness.

I've heard some pretty sharp guys refusing to believe in God argue love proves nothing. Their take is that because love is ultimately about what we can get out of the relationship it's only a survival mechanism. I actually agree with those guys. Love that is *only* about what we can get out of it isn't love at all. That's something else. It's not love.

My wife is as beautiful as she is amazing. But if I love my wife only because she cooks me dinner all the time and lets me snuggle on a cold night—that's not love. It's mutual survival. Love is not the by-product of a bazillion years of evolutionary and anthropological advancement. Real love is about more than survival. Real love is sacrificial.

Actual love is what it looks like to drag yourself out of bed before the sun comes up everyday because you're heading to work to provide for your family. Real love means setting aside your own wants and desires to make sure your kids have what they need. The kind of love that shows up when we're spending every day with Jesus is a lot different than the stuff in the movies. It's not about what we can get. It becomes about what we can give.

Two months after our conversation my friend Wes was driving home with his wife and three kids. They had been visiting the worksite where they were building their dream home when a drunk driver came speeding around the corner. At that terrible moment Wes had only a split second to react. Do you know what he did?

If love wasn't real—if it was only the result of an iterative survival mechanism etched out over millions of years, Wes would have done the opposite of what he actually did. Wes would not have turned the car at the last possible moment so that he and he alone took the full brunt of the terrible impact. But Wes did.

Why did Wes turn the car to take the hit? Because Wes believed in God. Wes spent everyday with Jesus. And all those days with Jesus–the easy ones and the hard ones, the beautiful ones and the ugly ones–had ingrained these words of Jesus in his heart, "no one has a greater love than this, laying down his own life for his friends."

Love is the biggest and best proof for God you can ever know. Because we were unlovable yet Jesus walked up that hill, and then stayed there for you and me. We were hopeless but Jesus came and willingly laid down his very life for our hope. Why? Why in the world would anyone do that? When Jesus' friend John struggled through hard times he remembered how Jesus himself answered the question, "because God loved the world so much he gave his only son".

Every devil in hell wants you to think you're not loved. Why? Because the existence of a real abiding, lasting, dependable love is proof God is real.

When my brother was dying I cried out to God who loves me. When my son was born and struggled to take his first breaths I hit my knees in prayer: crying out to a God who loves me. Someday I will surrender my last breath on this side of eternity. And I believe with everything I have my very next moment will put me face to face with Jesus. Why do I believe so strongly? Because I sense his love at work in my life everyday.

Love is the proof God is real. You just have to decide what you're willing to do about it.

CONCLUSION

For weeks my phone has been badgering me about the volume. Podcasts, audiobooks, music, and anything else my bluetooth keeps pumping out have apparently started setting it off. But I like to actually hear what I'm trying to hear. If I didn't want to hear it, I wouldn't turn it on in the first place. Does that mean I'm getting old?

I get why the guys at Apple decided our phones should warn us. Having something turned up too loud for too long isn't good for our ears. But what the software failed to consider was the interference between the place the sound begins (my phone) and the place it winds up (my head).

I hope the last 55,000 words were really loud for you. Not because I hope you'll have a headache. But because I'm convinced Jesus has been trying to remind you of them for a while. And he wants to cut through the noise.

Jesus wants us all to know that he is with us. He's

hoping we will follow right here and now. With his help he knows we can avoid a lot of the wrong turns seeking to get us lost. And Jesus knows that everyday with him will leave us satisfied like nothing else can.

We all have a cost to consider as we pursue a better savior than the ones we may have tried the first couple of times. None of that surprises Jesus. He considered it all before he ever started carrying his cross up that hill. He thought of you as he hung there.

Jesus stayed on his cross so you would put down your mask and find some friends to run with. He knew you would have to face off against some bad guys and didn't want you to tackle it alone. He certainly didn't want you to spend any time looking back over your shoulder in regret. Instead Jesus is reminding you how he'll help you see through the fog on your really hard days. He's assuring you of what can happen when you trust him a little longer for a better outcome.

Everyday with Jesus is meant to be a reminder of how he helps us find our way home. The place where he delights in who we are and how much he loves us. Jesus helps us know we don't have to get stuck in our bad habits. Walking with him was never meant to be complicated. It was always about going at it with the simplicity of everything we've got.

Everyday with Jesus is better than any day without him. Everyday without him. Living in his truth means living a better story. The kind he writes with you step for step. A story where we learn to pray about anything. It's a story where our love is louder than the noise. It's a story where life gets sweeter for anyone around us. Everyday with Jesus is a story about knowing God is real. Not because of the arguments someone made, but because of the love that gave everything up for you. The same love that has taken center stage in your heart.

Maybe you thought you simply reached the end of this book. Maybe you were thinking you would turn the page and go on to the next thing. Instead, I think what Jesus wants for us both is to see what's next.

Some of you reading this need to commit. You've stuck it out to the end of this book, but never taken a serious step toward a life with Jesus. Like Roger the soldier you showed up looking for help. Pray. Seriously. Just do it right now. Don't make it complicated. Make it happen. Tell Jesus you're ready.

Some of you have been walking with Jesus. Now it's time to turn it up a notch. Let his love be the loudest thing in your life everyday. You will never regret it.

This moment has come to a close for us both. Now it's time to write the next one. But we won't write it if we keep our eyes closed. It's time to look up and look out. We can't ignore what Jesus wants. We can't pretend he doesn't love us with a ridiculous, extravagant, universe shifting kind of love. We can't let our hands forget what our heart has come to know. See the people in your life that need to know the truth we've come to live by, everyday with Jesus is better than any day without him. What you do next is up to you.

Enjoy *Everyday Jesus*?

Check out other books by Nathan King.

The Wisdom Trail Guide:
31 Steps to a Life of Wisdom

Learn Love Live:
The Story God Wants For Your Life

Generational Generosity
(with Richard Rogers)

The Christmas Trail Guide:
25 Days of Advent

ABOUT THE AUTHOR

Nathan King lives with his family in Arkansas. You can find him hiking with his family, building something with his hands, or in his neighborhood walking his dog. He and Jamie have the distinct privilege of serving as pastors at New Life Church in Conway, AR. You can find him online at www.nathanking.com, YouTube.com/@TheBiblcShorts, tiktok.com/@nathanking.com. For speaking inquiries contact help@nathanking.com.

www.ingramcontent.com/pod-product-compliance
Lightning Source LLC
LaVergne TN
LVHW041540070426
835507LV00011B/838